Married to the Business

Honey I love you but our business sucks

Other books by Dr Greg Chapman:

The Five Pillars of Guaranteed Business Success:
Why Most Businesses Stay Small and What You can Do about Yours
www.FivePillarsBusinessSuccess.com

Price: How You can Charge More without Losing Sales
www.IncreaseYourPrices.com

MARRIED TO THE
BUSINESS

Honey I love you but our business sucks

Dr Greg Chapman

Married to the Business: Honey I love you but our business sucks
By Dr Greg Chapman
www.GregChapman.biz

Published by Empower Business Solutions Pty., Ltd.
Suite 22, 738 Burke Rd., Camberwell, Victoria, 3124, Australia
info@empowersolutions.com.au; http://www.empowersolutions.com.au
ABN 14 108 173 708

Order copies at: www.MarriedtotheBusiness.biz

Chapman, Greg
Married to the Business: Honey I love you but our business sucks
1st ed.
ISBN 978-0-9805059-2-4 (pbk.).
1. Success in business. 2. Small business - Growth. 3.
Small business - Management. 4. Business - Planning. 5.
Business. I. Title.

Disclaimer
The material contained in this publication is general only and has been prepared without taking into account your objectives, financial situation or needs. Certain assumptions have been made based on the general conditions for a typical user of this information. Such assumptions may or may not prove to be correct. Any forecasts based of this information and these assumptions may not be indicative of future performance which may vary greatly as a result of the foregoing. Accordingly, no representations are made to the accuracy, completeness or reasonableness of the statements, estimates and projections within this publication. Further, no responsibility is taken for omissions, errors or contrary interpretation of the information provided in this publication. Empower Business Solutions and its employees and professional advisors do not guarantee, whether expressly or implied, any results you may or may not get as a result of following our recommendations. This publication is provided on the basis that its recipient will carry out its own independent assessment of the information contained herein with its own advisors and make its own independent decisions on whether to implement the recommendations. Empower Business Solutions and its employees assume no responsibility or liability whatsoever on behalf of the client or reader of these materials.

Adherence to all applicable laws and regulations governing professional licensing, business practices, advertising and all other aspects of doing business in Australia, or any other jurisdictions, is the sole responsibility of the client.

Contents

Acknowledgements

While I have worked with businesses with a wide variety of ownership structures, and these experiences have provided an important foundation to my understanding of how small businesses can become successful, this book would not have been possible without my clients who are "Married to the Business".

Without doubt, the highs are higher, and the lows are lower with couples in business and navigating through these troubled waters is something I had to learn from experience and I thank these clients for allowing me to learn from them.

In particular I want to acknowledge one couple who provided the contents of the chapter "Emails to the Advisor". These were real emails to me from one client couple and have been included with their permission. I have edited them to fit the story, but the passion from the original emails remains untouched.

Thank you also to the people who reviewed the manuscript. Special mention for Geoff Haw who went above and beyond the call of duty.

Finally, I want to acknowledge my wife Helen who provided valuable feedback whilst I was engaged in writing this book. We are not "Married to the Business", as she has her own business and is an accomplished author. Any errors or faults remaining in this book are mine alone, and definitely not hers!

Foreword by Peter Strong

Executive Director
Council of Small Business Australia

In his latest book Dr Greg Chapman has embraced the world of small business in a way that reflects the huge change that has happened over the last two decades. The Australian business landscape is being overrun by small business people and many of these people are not just business partners, they are also life partners. Over 90% of businesses are small and over half of these do not employ any other people. There are some 2.5 million small business people in Australia.

For too long business 'experts' have focused on business processes and theories without looking at the basic nature of a small business. The reality is that a small business is a person and more often than not it will be two people trying to do their own thing and make their way through life in control of their destiny.

The people who are wed to a business and wed to each other offer our society a whole range of outcomes that need to be embraced. Not only are they part of the backbone of the economy, they are also the soul of any community. But the nature of couples is that they will often have offspring and those offspring, the future business people of Australia, will be educated in the best way possible on the good, the bad and the wonderful, of running your own business. They will be educated by their parents in the world of small business where there isn't theory – there is only fact; where everyday observation will give the young of small business couples a deep and ingrained understanding of the business world.

Greg's book investigates this real world – no big business theories here; and looks at what will confront many business people as they develop their business. He also investigates the relationship issues that will crop up and effect communications, decision making and planning. These are real issues that, if not dealt with effectively, can not only undermine a business, but can also undermine a healthy personal relationship.

Greg doesn't ignore issues around the strengths and weaknesses to be found in any relationship, both business and private. He is not afraid to suggest solutions to problems that may create some challenge for a relationship when the necessary decisions are to be made, but may also create opportunities and positive outcomes to be gained.

And the best advice from the book; seek expert advice from the right people. Make sure your advisers know the difference between a big business and a real life small business run by two people, with all the emotions and challenges that close relationships can present.

I congratulate Greg on another quality publication and look forward to further books on the largest most productive sector in Australian business, small business and the people in that business.

Peter Strong
Executive Director
Council of Small Business Australia

Preface

Small businesses come in a wide variety of shapes and sizes, varying from solo operations to businesses with up to fifty employees. They may have had one owner, or multiple owners. Where there were multiple owners, it is essential that they operate with a common purpose and speak with one voice.

A particular subgroup of multiple owner businesses is where the owners are in a personal as well as a business relationship. Over the years I have found that a significant proportion of my clients fall into this category. I also found that I greatly enjoyed working with these types of owners. Not because I see myself as some sort of marriage counsellor – I am most definitely not, and my wife will back me up on this, but because I enjoy working with the different perspectives each partner brings and the special regard they have for each other.

Where I have worked with client businesses with multiple owners but without a personal relationship, there have been instances where the owners were at loggerheads with each other and had totally conflicting visions for the business. It is very rare that I see this situation with couples "Married to the Business". Their vision tends to be shared, although there will be disagreements on how it should be achieved.

Even where there is a disagreement, there is a far greater keenness to see the other's point of view. It is rare one person is completely wrong or right, it is more that they don't have complete information or have not considered other ways of dealing with the differences. There is also additional supportiveness, and a strong desire for both to make things work- after all they have bet their relationship on it.

In a worst case situation, the pressure of running a business together can push the relationship to breaking point, but with the right advice, the pressure can be reduced and the enthusiasm they had when they first started working along side each other can return.

In working with both couples in business and with those businesses without a personal relationship between the partners, much of the advice I provide may be quite similar. However, there is an important difference in how to manage the business relationship in a way that does not impact on the personal one due to higher levels of sensitivity and investment in that relationship. For other types of business partnerships, at the end of the day the partners go back to different homes.

I found that I get an additional level of satisfaction seeing the great results achieved by my clients who are "Married to the Business"'. In other business partnerships, the most significant person in the owners' life does not directly see the changes and often do not understand the effort that client has made. When the effort is shared by their personal partner, enjoyment of the rewards is that much greater.

For me, I think this is why I enjoy working with clients who are "Married to the Business".

Dr Greg Chapman

Introduction

Of all business partnerships, the most intimate, in all senses of the word, are those where the owners are in a personal relationship.

Perhaps the biggest reason why these partnerships are different to other business partnerships is the very strong alignment of "Married to the Business" partners' life and business goals. They also have a level of trust that is rarely seen with other types of partnerships. It is possibly their greatest strength.

The long term commitment of the owners to the business is another strength. They often have a desire to build a business that they can pass onto the next generation, which becomes a real problem for partners not in a relationship. Many studies have shown that this long term view of business partners in a personal relationship results in greater profitability compared with other similar businesses.

There is also a greater pride of ownership in these businesses which reflects in the service quality, as their family name and reputation is inextricably tied to the business.

Tolerating each other's foibles far more than would occur for non-couple partners can also be an advantage in that minor deficiencies in the business relationship are less likely to blow out of control as the couple have far more invested in their relationship. However, this can be a two edged sword and can result in problems being ignored rather than being addressed at an early stage.

A further advantage for couples in business is that they can design their business to suit their lifestyle. The differing lifestyles and life goals of non-couple business partners can result in major disputes. After achieving a certain level of success, one partner may wish to continue to grow the business and keep up the hard work that achieved that success while the other partner may wish to reduce their work hours to enjoy life more. A couple is far more likely to resolve these issues together.

Flexibility of their shared working arrangements is another advantage for "Married to the Business" partners. In the event of one partner of a couple being unable to work for an extended period, the other will take on the extra burden for the benefit of both. For non-couple partners, unless covered by insurance, a partner will likely be resentful if their partner is not pulling their weight and is still drawing funds from the business and holding their share of the business.

There are, however, downsides to these partnerships. Primarily the blurred line between objectivity and emotional responses when issues arise. Of course this occurs with all types of partnerships. Where there is no personal relationship this could be as a result of different life objectives of the partners. In the case of differences between couples in business together, who want the same things for their life, this can be all the more painful.

The flip side of trust, which is a strength with partners in a relationship, is that this encourages informality. This can result in a lack of discipline and reporting because, after all, the partners trust each other, but without effective reporting systems, it is difficult for a business to prosper.

While this book is called "Married to the Business", there are other types of personal relationships than only those that are a result of a marriage ceremony. This book is for any partnership where there is a strong personal as well as a business bond, even if it is only friendship.

While the prevalence of couples in business partnerships has been poorly documented, estimates are that up to 70% of businesses are family businesses. As this includes father and son and other types of relationships, the numbers of those "Married to the Business" will be less than this number, but it is clear that as a proportion of all businesses the numbers will still be very significant.

There are several ways that these business partnerships can arise, but the following are the three most typical arrangements.

Professional Peers

A very common situation is that the couple meets while undertaking the same course at university, and when they graduate, they start their own joint practice. Alternatively, they may be working in similar roles in a large organisation and decide to leave and start their own business utilising the skills they have both developed in their early careers. This type of partnership is distinguishable from others by both partners having professional skills that are directly relevant to delivering the core services of the business.

Examples of this are architects who start their own practice or a Human Resources agency where one partner may be in recruiting and the other in training.

Non-Professional Peers

While similar to Professional Peers, in this case the couple may not have any professional training relevant to the core service, but wanted to go into business together, possibly buying a business in which they can both work. The skills these businesses require have lower barriers to entry than professional businesses but require hard work and potentially long hours. That is not to say that no training is required, but the knowledge may by be attained through a short course or on the job from the previous owner.

An example of this type of business might be opening a café or running a graphic design/printing business.

Specialist and Non-Specialist – Non-Peers

In this case one of the partners has a specialist skill, often a trade and the other has more of a support role. The second partner may manage the office, schedule appointments and keep the books. A key difference in this relationship to the others is that the non-specialist does not have a deep understanding of the specialist's area of skill, so they have to refer most of the client questions to their specialist partner.

An example of this type of business might be a plumbing business or even a medical practice with the non-specialist partner as the practice manager.

Of all the business types, the specialist/non–specialist partnership is the most difficult arrangement. If the partners were not "Married to the Business", they would unlikely to be partners at all. In fact, the specialist would own the business, and hire an employee to be the office manager.

Other Business Partnerships

Whatever the business ownership arrangement, the need for vision, structure, systems, reporting and governance is just as important, and while some of the conflict examples within this book may not be relevant for non-couple partners, the strategies within this book are applicable for almost any business partnership arrangement.

Married to the Business: Case Study

The specialist/non-specialist partnership was chosen as the case study of this book because the differences are more extreme between the partners.

This does not mean that these issues do not exist in the peer partnerships. On the contrary, all good business partnerships are a combination of complimentary skills rather than a duplication of skills. In fact, many business partnerships fail where the partners have very similar skill sets and preferred ways of operating. For example, they both prefer the big picture and neither likes to do the detailed work that is also necessary.

If it is true that opposites attract in personal relationships, it means that they have a head start when they start a business together!

So even if the partners are peers, it is very common for one of them to have a much greater interest in the business side and the other to be more of a technician. An example of this is in a design business where one partner has a greater creative flair while the other is better at managing the creative process and making sure that the business results are achieved. Often one partner enjoys selling and the other just wants to deliver the service that first one sells.

The split between preferences for a technical or business focus is certainly more common in the specialist/non–specialist partnership and more obvious, but is still prevalent in most other partnership types. The different perspectives these preferences produce cause many of the tensions in the business partnership.

Gender Stereotypes

While "Married to the Business" might appear to exclude non male/female relationships, this is not meant to be the case, as this book focuses on roles, not genders. However the case study will be based on a male/female partnership, because that is by far the most common.

With the focus on a specialist/non-specialist relationship, a gender had to be assigned for the case study. In the modern world, there are a large number of examples where the specialist role is female, but again, by dint of numbers, given the overwhelming number of trades people are male, the specialist role in the case study has been assigned to a male.

Author's Note: *I have had clients where the female has been the specialist, but it has been mostly males with the female initiating contact to get advice. Is that because most men don't think they need help or am I gender stereotyping again?*

Being "Married to the Business"

While it is common that both partners in a marriage work, only a few work in the same business, and specifically one that they own jointly. Far more common is that couples work in different businesses, or one partner may own and operate a business without the involvement of their spouse.

Owning a business is very different from being an employee. Owners are legally responsible for the solvency of the business, and don't have the rights of an employee. In fact, it's the owner's responsibility to ensure that the employees receive all their entitlements, irrespective of whether their business is making money. Too often the owner is the last person to be paid. For employees, all this is someone else's problem. All they need to do is turn up on time and do what they are told.

When both partners of a couple own and work in the business, the business income may be the only income the couple receives. When there is pressure on the business financially, there is a big temptation for one member of the couple to get a job while the other struggles to keep the business going.

Where only one partner is involved in the business, as long as the other makes sufficient money for the couple's lifestyle, the first partner has a free hand in decision making, irrespective of the quality of the decisions.

However, if the business is the main source of income for the family, but doesn't provide the lifestyle desired, the non-involved partner may feel a need to participate more in decision making – particularly on spending decisions and where they see inefficiencies.

Apart from financial pressures, there will always be disagreements on how the business should be run. Where partners are not "Married to the Business", their disagreements can be resolved far more objectively, without crossing over to other issues affecting their personal lives.

Unfortunately, pressures can become so great that divorces can occur, but it is usually just the straw that breaks the camel's back, not the instigator of the breakdown.

> *The Appendix of this book discusses the impact of divorce on businesses previously owned by partners "Married to the Business".*

The right advice can defuse the pressures of partners "Married to the Business" if the commitment and good will between them still exists and that they are prepared to take the journey together, if someone will show them the path.

Action Steps

Provided at the end of this book are Action Steps for readers keen to implement the strategies and follow journey of the couple "Married to the Business" in this Case Study. These Action Steps will refer to key chapters within the book where pivotal actions are taken by the couple.

Some of the steps will refer to worksheets and documents for which access details are provided on the Resources page of this book.

Not all these steps will be applicable to every business, but for couples "Married to the Business" who decide to make no changes after reading this book, they should acknowledge that they are resigning themselves to the situation that currently exists in their business. That is, they are happy with the way things are now. If that is not the case, the challenge for them is:

What will you change to change your outcomes?

Chapter 1

Meet the Taylors

Luke Taylor first met Anna while he was working as a carpenter for Bill Jackson, a house builder. Bill's company Jackson Construction generally managed five projects at a time. Bill's Office Manager was his daughter Gail and Anna worked in the office.

Anna had joined Jackson's just as Luke had been promoted to site supervisor for one of Bill's projects. As site supervisor, he was also responsible for reporting to the office on the project he was managing, providing all the data that Bill required to run the business. The person with whom Luke spent most time in the office was Anna, who was responsible for collating the data from each site and producing reports for Bill.

Luke and Anna hit it off straight away, and before too long Luke was asking Anna out after work. Within a year, Luke had proposed to Anna, and she accepted. Bill was so pleased, that he threw an engagement party for the couple. Everyone from the business was there along with all their friends and family.

While Luke and Anna enjoyed working at Jackson's, they could see that Bill's business was not going to expand. In fact, Bill often revealed how satisfied he was with his business. He was clearly doing well. He had four cars, one of which was a Porsche. His wife, Jenny, didn't need to work, his kids were at private schools, and he regularly spent time at his hobby farm in the country where he spent his time fishing and water skiing.

One other thing Luke noticed about Bill; the only time he swung a hammer nowadays was on his hobby farm. He preferred spending his time sourcing clients and running the business.

Bill was enjoying himself too much, Luke decided. If he were to get ahead, he would have to leave Jackson's.

This was a major decision, and he and Anna spent many hours discussing this together. It was a risk to leave, but Luke had enough experience to become a registered builder and Anna knew enough to manage the office of a builder.

While life was comfortable at Jackson's, Anna encouraged Luke to make the leap. Although they wanted kids, it was still just the two of them and as Anna said, "Luke, it is now or never. We can't depend on Bill for the rest of our careers and if we leave it too late and Bill decides to retire or sell up we might have to start again at a time that mightn't be right for us."

Luke agreed but was still worried. "Neither of us has run a business before and while we have money put away, it probably won't last us more than a year."

Anna was more confident. "Sitting in the office over the last few years, I got a pretty good idea how Bill and Gail run the business, and I think within a year we should be able to start turning a profit. I'm excited about this. It will be our business. You'll look after the building, and I'll look after the money," she said with a laugh.

By this time, Luke was starting to share Anna's confidence and enthusiasm. "Okay," Luke said. "When should we give our notice?" he grinned, "and when can I order my Porsche?"

Anna became serious again. "I think we have to plan this out before we jump into this. After all, do you know how we will find our first client?"

Chapter 2

The Journey Begins

The first step was an obvious one. Luke had to become registered as a builder. He also looked at how he could build their first house. There were many sub-contractors that Bill used in his business that worked on other projects as well. Luke knew who the good ones were. He worked out how he would put a team together. He also knew he would have to be on the tools himself.

Meanwhile, Anna was thinking about how the business was to be run, and where they might find that first client. She decided, to keep costs down, they would run things from home. Bill had a well designed office, but they would not be able to afford anything like that. A computer, printer, fax and phone in the back bedroom was all she would need.

Anna was still stumped about the first client. She saw what Bill did. Most of his clients were from referrals. That was not going to work for a new business, but she knew sometimes Bill referred clients to others if he was too busy, or did not want to take the job for other reasons. Perhaps she could persuade Bill to refer to them, although she was not sure about his reaction when they finally told him about their decision.

She knew Bill did a small amount of advertising and attracted some enquiries through his website. He also sponsored the local football team, which seemed also to generate enquiries.

Anna decided that the best strategies to start would be a website, advertising in their local paper and speaking with other builders they knew, to see if they would refer them business they did not want.

After discussing their plans, Anna and Luke agreed that they were as ready as they would ever be. The following day they both gave their notice to Bill.

Bill was initially surprised about their decision, because he thought they were both happy at Jackson's, but gradually saw it was the logical step for them both. Anna thought he might be angry that they might steal his clients as a competitor. Bill laughed. "It is going to be quite a while before you are my competition, but I wish you the best of luck. And if you really want my client cast-offs you are more than welcome, but you might not thank me for it!"

So Taylor Construction was born.

In the beginning it was tough. The initial enquiries through their website were for small jobs which even if they got to the quote stage they didn't get the job. The newspaper ads seemed to generate no interest at all.

Luke and Anna were starting to get worried. This changed when they got a call from someone who said Bill gave them their name because he was too busy. The job was a reasonable size renovation of an old property. They got the job, probably, they felt, because Luke made sure it was a good price.

Anna rang up Bill to thank him for the referral, but Bill said ominously "Don't thank me yet". Nevertheless, she still thanked Bill and encouraged him to send others their way and let other builders know they could handle the overflow.

Luke assembled his team, and started the job for the client. The first problem he had was matching the materials with the existing structure. It was possible to locate them, but Luke found they were much more expensive than he had allowed. There were alternatives, but the client insisted that the renovation match the original structure as closely as possible.

As they proceeded with the demolition, they uncovered structural problems in areas that were not part of the original scope. The council insisted they had to be rectified before building could continue, and Anna found that the owner could not, or would not pay for these additional works. They had a choice – either pull out of the job, and end up with a legal fight on their first job, or just swallow the cost and complete the works.

Anna and Luke discussed the problem and worked out the costs. The extra works would mean that their profit would be wiped out and they would not be able to pay themselves for the job. They looked at their finances, and agreed they could afford to support themselves without any income from the job. They agreed it was important to get their first job completed, and they hoped that if the client understood what they would do for him, he would give them a great testimonial and refer other clients.

It didn't quite work out that way. Every milestone payment was late. The client was always changing his mind about details. There seemed nothing Luke could do that would make him happy. Completing the punch list for the final payment was a nightmare, but in the end the job was completed, and looked fantastic.

Anna rang hopefully a month later to ask how they liked their newly renovated home and get a testimonial. Instead she got an earful about 'blemishes' in the woodwork. It didn't matter that using original timbers meant that these imperfections were to be expected, compared with modern manufactured products. Anna felt deflated, that all their work was for nothing.

When Luke came home she told him what had happened. "Why, that ungrateful bastard," he said. It was all Anna could do to stop Luke driving around to the former client to give him a piece of his mind.

"What do we do now?" asked Anna.

"Well, I could call up Bill to thank him," Luke thought out loud. "Anyway, the architect thought we did a great job, and wants us to tender for another project."

Taylor Construction did bid on the next project for the architect. This time Luke took a lot more care in the budget estimate and made sure that there was sufficient margin to pay their wages. They won the project, and continued to work for this architect and for others to whom they were introduced by him.

Their first project was a near death experience, but they survived and so Anna and Luke became "Married to the Business".

Chapter 3

For Richer or Poorer

Seven years later Taylor Construction always seemed to be busy. They would generally have two to three projects on the go at a time. Anna had moved the office out of the spare bedroom (they would soon need it for a second addition to their family). Luke had built a stand alone office for her and her assistant in their large back yard with a play area for their son, Mark and the baby when it arrived.

Anna loved this arrangement. The best of all worlds, being able to be with Mark, and still being able to run the office, with the help of her assistant, Sally, who could cover for her when Mark needed attention.

Luke now had 6 full time staff, including a supervisor plus a team of subcontractors he could call on as he needed.

Together Anna and Luke had learnt a lot about the building business, and that building was only one part of it. They had made their fair share of mistakes, but they were getting a reasonable number of jobs now, although they realised it was a lot of work. Over the years they had many happy clients. Their first client now just seemed a distant nightmare.

While from the outside it looked like it was all going well, Anna, as the person who managed the finances, knew the business was not as great as her husband told everyone it was. Every week Anna had a pile of invoices to pay, not to mention making payroll for their staff, and then from what was left they drew their own wages. Sometimes there was nothing left.

When she discussed this with Luke, he just said, "I can't work any harder," and while she knew this to be true, she believed that Luke needed to prioritise more, and be less on call to everyone else. Some days he got nothing done that contributed to their cash flow and yet each night he came home exhausted.

Anna was frustrated, as, although they had been operating for all that time, nothing seemed to improve. In fact, they were barely better off now financially than when they worked for Bill, plus now they had a lot more worries.

They had no great problems finding the next job, even though sometimes, they didn't know where it would come from, something always seemed to turn up. However at the end of the month, at the end of the year, there was not enough left for them for all their effort.

Looking at the future and their growing family, Anna felt trapped by the business which seemed to be going nowhere, something even Luke admitted after one hard month when Anna showed him their bank statement.

They had been struggling with a particularly difficult project, where payments had been delayed due to milestones not being reached as a result of construction problems and cost blow-outs. Anna suggested they needed a hard look at how they were doing.

Did the business have a future? Should they try to find jobs? Anna could probably get work as an office manager, and Luke could probably find work as a supervisor for another contractor. Taylor Construction sometimes acted as subcontractors for other builders when Luke needed to keep his team together and he couldn't find a client himself. They made almost nothing on such jobs.

Luke also considered what his future working for someone else might look like. "You know most builders' businesses are pretty much like ours, and if I worked for someone else, there would be no guarantee the job would last," he observed. "Bill is the only builder I know who has done it right, but I hear he is semi-retired and only comes into town once a month to check the books. You know Gail runs the business now?"

"That doesn't surprise me," said Anna. "Did you know that Bill made her do a carpentry apprenticeship and work out on-site for a few years before he allowed her to become the office manager?" Anna had admiration for her old boss and friend. "Gail knew almost as much about the building business as Bill. I guess it was in her blood. Gail was the son Bill never had."

Luke had thought about going back to work with Bill or Gail, but it would be like admitting failure and going backwards and he didn't want to work for any of the other builders he knew. He had seen enough failures in the industry. He wanted to be in control and not dependent on the poor decisions of others.

Anna, on the other hand, could not see how they could go on like this. Their cupboard, while not bare was definitely not going to be restocked any time soon. The only way forward she could see was that she would get a job after the baby, and Luke could continue to run the business himself.

Luke was shocked that Anna would think of abandoning their business like this, but realised that they were running out of alternatives. "What would it take," Luke asked, "for you to continue to help me in our business?"

Anna thought for a moment before answering. "I need to see a plan. I need to see that you know how to turn this around into something that will support our family at least as well as a job. Doing what we are doing now is not a plan I can accept."

Luke looked crushed. "I don't have a plan," he finally admitted. "I don't know what to do next."

Anna touched his arm and gently suggested, "We need to get advice. Why don't you give Bill a call?"

Luke hesitated. He was unsure what Bill might say. They still kept in touch, Christmas cards and the odd phone call but Bill seemed to be having way too much fun to worry about business, but what had he to lose?

When he called Bill, he clearly was pleased to hear Luke's voice. After initial pleasantries, Luke let him know why he called.

"I'm sorry to hear you're having problems," Bill said. "Why don't you, Anna and Mark come down to the farm next weekend. It would be great to see you again. Jenny and I would love the company and it would give us the chance to talk."

ॐ

Luke and Anna had never been up to Bill's farm. He raised sheep on the property. "They're much easier to manage than cows, and are good at keeping the grass under control," he said.

There was a shed that contained all their farm machinery and Bill and Jenny's cars. "Just Land Rovers I see," said Luke. "What happened to the Porsche?"

Bill laughed. "Ah, my shiny toy. It's no good up here so I gave it to Gail. She loves it. Anyway there are plenty of other boy toys for me here on the farm."

While Bill was showing Luke around, Anna was listening to Jenny's stories of life on the farm. At times it got a little lonely, but there was always plenty to do, and once a month they drove into town for a few days to see Gail and her children, and Bill would spend time with Gail talking business, but they were always pleased to return to the peace of the farm.

When the men returned, Jenny organised everyone to help prepare lunch. It was quite a feast, including, of course, a roast lamb and salads and vegetables grown on the farm. Jenny and Bill were very proud of that. Bill had also a few grape vines on the property and had produced a quite reasonable wine from the grapes.

After lunch Anna started to describe their situation. She explained that managing their cash flow is their biggest problem. "I try to explain to Luke the cash flow problems, but he isn't that interested as we always seem to be able to scrape by. Luke gets much more excited seeing his projects go from the drawing board into bricks and mortar reality. He's a technician and a perfectionist. The clients love him."

"Apart from that very first client you sent us, Bill!" interjected Luke, smiling.

Bill looked sheepish. "I did say when I referred him to you not to thank me yet."

"Yeah, well, thanks for that referral. The client from hell." Luke was still smiling. "I mean it Bill, thank you. It was quite a learning curve."

"It forced us to realise that being a good builder is not enough to have a good building business," Anna added. "We changed a lot of things after him."

Luke then confessed to Bill, "Do you know this is the first weekend I've taken off in months? I nearly didn't come, but I did because Anna pushed me, but I'm glad she did. I spend all my days chasing contractors, organising suppliers, fixing problems on-site and talking to clients and when I come home, Anna asks whether I have followed up on enquiries and done the quotes. I end up doing them on weekends. I have three at home waiting on my desk right now.

"Anna gets frustrated because all these things are technical, and she can't answer the questions. I have to, but I just don't have the time. Then Anna shows me each month that we're losing money on jobs."

"I actually don't tell him the half of it," Anna added. "Luke's right, I don't understand the technical side of the business, and I have to rely on him so much. I do think he's spending more time than he needs to satisfy clients' every whim. He's way too accommodating. It just encourages them to keep asking for more. Often it's easier to agree with him to keep the peace, but at the same time I can see that the business isn't going anywhere."

It was clear that Anna was becomingly increasingly frustrated.

"I've never said this before, but I'm worried about my inability to get Luke to see what's wrong, and it's affecting our relationship. I even suggested he run the business himself, and I'd get a job so at least we could have a better standard of living."

Jenny hugged Anna, and empathised "That was how it was for Bill and I. Years ago, I worked with Bill in the business in the same way that you are with Luke, with similar results."

"What did you do?" asked Anna.

"Jenny told me I needed to get advice, or she'd have nothing to do with the business," Bill explained quietly. "It was the best thing she ever said to me about our business. I didn't want to lose her support as I couldn't run it without her. So we started looking for an advisor to assist us. This was before the Internet, so it took some time.

"I did ask our accountant if he could help, but I found he was really good at only one thing, tax. Eventually I found a professional business advisor who could cover not just our finances, but also help fix our operations and our marketing. Over the years we've had several advisors as our needs changed.

"If it was just me and the advisor, I'm not sure how many of the changes would have happened, but Jenny took to it like a duck to water. She loves the business stuff. She totally changed the way we ran the business, taking the advice and actually acting on it. I had to change the way I worked as well. Some of it was easy, some of it was tough. It probably took one to two years before we had things working the way we wanted.

"I think it was easier for Jenny than it was for me. She understood the problems far better than I and she could see how the solutions from our advisor would work pretty much straight away. For me, I thought I was going to lose control." Bill paused and gave a small laugh. "What control? I wasn't controlling anything. I was in constant damage limitation mode. The biggest thing stopping our business improving was my insisting that I control every detail, which was impossible. I was causing as many problems as I was fixing.

"As Jenny started to implement the new way of operating, things started to get easier, but they were never easy. I saw the benefits, and slowly became sold on them, although we still had disagreements. As the business grew, our systems had to grow with it, and we both had to get smarter. And that's when we really started making money, and all the hard work started to pay off."

Jenny took over the story. "We both had to change, not just Bill. Some of the new ideas were so simple, while others took a lot more effort. As we put the changes in place we found we could depend a lot more on our staff, but we had to show them the way. Then Gail expressed an interest to come into the business. Gail was just like Bill, and loved building things. Her first construction was when she helped Bill build her cubby house and later she helped with our extension.

"Bill and I discussed her going into the business and agreed she could end up running it, but she had to start from the ground up. We wanted her to do a trade. She always wanted to be a carpenter like Bill, but we also wanted her to understand what happened in the office. She had the education we wished we'd had, and after a while she started coming to our board meetings. That was about the time I had a series of medical problems, and Bill and I agreed that I would withdraw from the business and get my health back, and let Gail take over from me.

"I was still able to come in from time to time and give her a hand, and offer advice, but basically, she took over just by following the systems Bill and I had created. As she learnt them, she looked for ways to improve them, especially bringing in technology, which neither of us were very good at. Once my health returned, I didn't want to go back to work, and I didn't need to. Gail was reigning supreme. We are both so proud of her."

"My only involvement nowadays," Bill continued "is our monthly boardrooms which Gail likes as it forces her to be accountable, and she bounces ideas off me in a formal way. But other than that, she's the boss!"

"I had no idea you went through the same things we did," said Anna. "Everything seemed to work so smoothly when I was there. So smoothly, I totally underestimated what it took to get to that level control. So you think we should get our own advisor?"

"Yes," Jenny nodded. "Do your research, and find someone whose philosophy and style suits you. It is important that you like them, but you know they are not there to be your friend, and there will be some tough love. At least you have Google now so finding an experienced and well qualified advisor is a whole lot easier."

"What about you, Bill?" inquired Luke a little nervously. "Would you be our advisor?"

Bill shook his head. "Asking friends to be your advisor can end in tears. What happens if the advice doesn't work for you, or you don't implement it the right way, or you don't implement it at all? What would a friend do then? I am sure your other friends are giving advice to you all the time. How much have you acted on?

"Friends are well meaning, and will accept your excuses for not following their advice. An advisor you pay is not there to be your friend, although they may become one, but not before they tell you some things you may not want to hear. But you will listen, because you are paying them. If they are any good, they will also tell you what you need to hear without making you over defensive, so you'll continue to listen.

"There'll be some hard feedback. They've heard all the excuses before, and you've paid them to get results. And if you don't follow their advice, you know you're wasting your money, and they'll tell you that. On the other hand, if you think their advice is no good, you can sack them. Now good ones aren't cheap, but what value do you place on turning your business around? I've given you the advice I feel comfortable giving, but now the rest is up to you."

"Thank you both for sharing your experiences with us," responded Luke nodding slowly. "We'll start searching next week, but in the mean time, may I have another glass of that rather interesting Chateau d'William?"

Go to the Action Steps section for this Chapter now

Chapter 4

A New Beginning

It took about a month of researching, and after talking with several advisors, they chose one that they both liked and in whom they had confidence. Luke was concerned about the cost, but Anna did some calculations and showed Luke that if the advisor only increased their turnover by 10%, this would be more than a 400% return on investment for just one year.

"And we should be able to keep that extra turnover, years after we finish with the advisor. I don't think it's a big risk," Anna stated. "Anyway do we really have an alternative?"

On the day of their first meeting, they were both nervous and excited by the possibilities.

The Advisor asked many questions about their business and the issues they faced. Anna went through the same things she had gone over with Bill and Jenny. Cash flow was always a problem, she explained, and Luke seemed to be spending all his time in damage control.

After listening for some time, the Advisor said, "It's always an issue to know where to start, and ideally we would attack all the problems at once, but when you do that nothing gets completed. I suggest we start with your cash flow issues. After all, Cash is King in any business. Many businesses go broke making a profit. So let's start off with your Profit and Loss statement."

Anna printed one off from her computer, but it was two months old. The Advisor said, "This is one of the first things that must change. Your target is to have your monthly financial report by the end of the first week of the following month. Otherwise it's like trying to drive a car by only looking through the rear vision mirror."

Anna started to explain. "With all the constant interruptions, it's hard to enter all the data, and Luke has to check the invoices and the accounts from suppliers before we send them ....."

The Advisor interrupted. "To get different results, we'll need to do things differently. That means simple systems so that Luke doesn't need to review everything. All these invoices and accounts are entirely predictable. Invoices are based on your contracts, and accounts are based on orders that Luke makes and delivery dockets. So office staff should be able to undertake 90% of the review process on Luke's behalf. You just need some rules to be followed. Now about this Profit and Loss Statement."

At that point, Luke's phone rang. "Excuse me, I have to take this," he said.

After Luke had finished his call he looked up to see the Advisor frowning at him. "Was that a medical emergency?" the Advisor asked sharply.

"No" answered Luke.

"Was it something that could've waited an hour?"

"I guess so," Luke admitted. "I've been trying to talk with this client since yesterday about a change he wanted, but it could have waited an hour."

"In future, when I'm here, I want Sally to screen your calls, with only emergency calls being allowed through while we are working on your business. Do you think the CEO of a bank would interrupt her board meeting for similar calls? It is rare that anything is a true emergency. Most things can wait a few hours. Don't let others control your time. Is that clear Luke and Anna?"

They nodded.

"Okay, let's get back to your Profit and Loss statement. Correct me if I'm wrong, but it doesn't appear that either of you are drawing a regular wage. Is that right?"

"That's right," Anna admitted. "We have to balance what we take out for ourselves against paying our staff and creditors, so our wages are up and down – what's left at the end of the month really. The net profits are our wages."

The Advisor made some notes on the statement and then looked up. "What I am seeing here is quite typical for couples in business. Neither is getting paid what they would receive if they were doing the same jobs for someone else. Its worse with both partners working in the business because that usually means that money may be their whole income. At least if one partner has a separate job, they can support the other in the business. How much do you think you really need to live comfortably?"

"At least 50% more than we earned together last year. It was a real struggle," Anna replied.

Luke interjected, "But if we do that we'll have to put up our prices and we're struggling as it is."

"You really don't have a choice," said the Advisor, "because at the moment, your business is not sustainable. You must set a reasonable income for yourselves as a family that meets your lifestyle needs. If your business can't provide that for you, why on earth would you have a business? In any case, it may not just mean you have to put up your prices; you may also be able to reduce your costs. I see a lot of wastage in what you're currently doing. Ideally you'll do both. Also, you're not depreciating assets of your business."

Taylor Construction Profit & Loss - Last 12 months	
Sales	**1,619,600**
Labour	336,730
Subcontractors	274,220
Materials	699,780
Gross Profit	**308,870**
Overheads	
Advertising	5,750
Dues & Fees	11,920
Equipment Costs	6,775
Insurances	22,275
Labour	59,050
Office Expenses	18,540
Telephones and IT	4,250
Vehicle Costs	26,420
Vehicle Leases	56,380
Other Expenses	13,570
Total Overheads	**224,930**
Net Profit	**83,940**

"Our accountant takes care of that when she does our tax," said Anna.

"I'm sure she does, but you need to recover the cost of these assets over their lifetime in your Profit and Loss through your pricing. When you include both items, you can see what appears as a break even business is really a loss making one. That's why you always struggle."

"Oh my," Anna gasped. "That's why."

Luke was still confused. "When I create a quote for a new project, I always make sure we have a good margin. How can it end up like this?"

"Look, I'll show you," the Advisor explained. "This is your Profit and Loss statement as it is now. I will put in $120,000 for your combined wages split say 50:50. When we look at your time Luke, how much of it is spent directly on construction? That excludes the time you spend with Anna running the business."

Luke thought for a few moments. "I guess about 80%," he said.

Anna agreed.

"Now, this won't change your bottom line at all, but I'm going to include those costs with your direct labour, to give us the total Cost of Goods Sold so we can properly calculate your Gross Profit," said the Advisor. "That way, if you double the number of houses you build, you'll double your Gross Profit. Obviously you'd need more labour to do that. Does that make sense?" They both nodded in agreement.

The Advisor paused briefly. "Your original Profit & Loss statement excludes Luke's labour costs from the Gross Profit. The last step is to put in your depreciation. To keep things simple, let's say you have about $150,000 of assets, which would include the one vehicle you told me you own rather than lease, and the value of the office, which you don't charge yourselves rent on, and its equipment. Again, to keep things simple, let's say the average life of these assets is 5 years. That means that your annual depreciation before net profit is $30,000. This is what it looks like with these adjustments, and is much closer to reality."

"Luke, can you see it now?" asked Anna.

Luke sighed. "What can we do?"

Taylor Construction Profit & Loss - Last 12 months Adjusted by Advisor	
Sales	**1,619,600**
Labour incl. Luke's direct labour	384,730
Subcontractors	274,220
Materials	699,780
Gross Profit	**260,870**
Overheads	
Advertising	5,750
Dues & Fees	11,920
Equipment Costs	6,775
Insurances	22,275
Labour incl. Luke & Anna admin.	131,050
Office Expenses	18,540
Telephones and IT	4,250
Vehicle Costs	26,420
Vehicle Leases	56,380
Other Expenses	13,570
Total Overheads	**296,930**
Depreciation	30,000
Net Profit	**-66,060**

"We work backwards," the Advisor replied. "Let's start with a net profit of 5% of your current Sales. That's $80,000. A 10% net profit would be better, but let's not be too ambitious. Remember, this will be profit after you have paid yourselves a decent wage. We add back your Depreciation and your overheads. I'm also going to take the liberty of including my fees for the rest of the year," the Adviser smiled, "and we discover the Gross Profit you need is around $430,000."

"That's about 40% more than we're making now, even before paying ourselves what we should. How would that be possible?" Anna wondered.

The Advisor looked at Luke. "I think there's a lot of waste in your construction cost, particularly your time. Could you reduce your costs, including your time by 10%?"

"I'm not too sure about that," Luke answered.

"What about 5%?" countered the Advisor.

"Okay,' Luke conceded. "That shouldn't be too hard."

Taylor Construction
Profit & Loss - with Increased Margins

Sales	**1,710,000**
Labour	360,000
Subcontractors	260,000
Materials	660,000
Gross Profit	**430,000**
Overheads	
Advertising	5,750
Dues & Fees incl. Advisor	35,000
Equipment Costs	6,775
Insurances	22,275
Labour	131,050
Office Expenses	18,540
Telephones and IT	4,250
Vehicle Costs	26,420
Vehicle Leases	56,380
Other Expenses	13,570
Total Overheads	**320,010**
Depreciation	30,000
Net Profit	**79,990**

"And do you think anyone would notice if you increased your prices by 5%, especially if you could convince people about the quality of your building?" asked the Advisor.

"We could do that," agreed Anna.

"Well, if you could make both those changes, that would be sufficient to give you the target Gross Profit $430,000 which will get you up to 5% net profit. Obviously these numbers are rough and you should fine tune them, but we're not finished yet. Luke, you're currently building five houses a year. With better management could you increase that to six?"

"That might be a bit harder, but it's not impossible. In fact there are probably a lot of things we could do better," Luke agreed.

The Advisor spent several minutes recalculating their Profit and Loss statement. "This is what it would look like if you just reduced costs by 5%, increased prices by 5% and built one more house per year. Not only will you be paying yourselves a decent wage, recovered the cost of your assets, you would be left with a Net Profit of $165,000 after your $120,000 joint wages. How do you feel about that?"

"That's amazing!" Anna exclaimed.

Luke stared at the numbers the Advisor had written out for them and grinned. "Is it really as easy as that?"

The Advisor laughed. "No, there's still a lot of hard work, but what I wanted to do is to show you that it was not an impossible task. Before we see these sets of numbers in your accounts, there's several changes you'll have to make to the way you operate, but one thing you can do straight away is add 5% to your prices. The other things will take a little longer."

Before he left, the Advisor provided them with a list of tasks he wanted them to complete – he called them homework – before their next meeting. They were to call him if they needed help beforehand, and unless there was an emergency, he expected them to complete the tasks. Anna assured him they would do their homework.

Taylor Construction Profit & Loss - with Margin & Productivity Increases	
Sales	2,052,000
Labour	431,999
Subcontractors	312,000
Materials	792,000
Gross Profit	**516,000**
Overheads	
Advertising	5,750
Dues & Fees	35,000
Equipment Costs	6,775
Insurances	22,275
Labour	131,050
Office Expenses	18,540
Telephones and IT	4,250
Vehicle Costs	26,420
Vehicle Leases	56,380
Other Expenses	13,570
Total Overheads	**320,010**
Depreciation	30,000
Net Profit	**165,990**

After he had gone, Luke and Anna looked at each other "Wow," said Luke. "I didn't expect that."

"It's a bit scary," admitted Anna, "but to think the answer was out there all the time if we'd only known to ask the right person."

"It feels like we're starting the business all over again, but this time the way we should've in the first place." Luke smiled.

Anna started to hug Luke when Sally came in, telling Luke, "Oh sorry to interrupt, but it's that client on the phone again."

Go to the Action Steps section for this Chapter now

Chapter 5

Time to Act

At their next meeting with their advisor, Anna had to admit that they had not done much of their homework. "We had computer problems and we had to re-enter last month's data into our bookkeeping program, on top of completing this month's as well. And Luke was really busy with a new client."

The Advisor was not surprised. "I rather suspected this would happen, but I wanted to make sure that this was the case. We should probably spend a while today talking about managing your time. How productive do you feel you are each day? By productive, I mean doing what you plan to do and not just busy."

Luke just laughed. "If I get half of what I planned to do in a day done, I think I've had a great day. I get interrupted all the time by clients, the office, suppliers, and sub-contractors. So the only time I get to do the office work Anna needs me to do is at nights and on weekends, which doesn't do much for our home life."

"It's much the same with me," said Anna. "Chasing clients for money, chasing suppliers to correct their invoices and wiping the nose of the boys on-site, who never seem to be able to get their act together. Then I have to chase Luke to get him to answer questions about almost everything. Then to top it all off, Mark has been sick."

"Well, I've had other things on my mind as well," added Luke. "Some products we needed for a job were unavailable, and I had to find a new supplier. I've been one man down on one project as I had to fire someone for repeated shoddy work. It just never stops."

"Well it has to if we're to get anywhere," the Advisor stated. "You need to distinguish the urgent from the important. Let me show you how. From what you've told me, so far, there was only one thing that affected your business that was both important and urgent. That was attending to Mark. All the other things you mentioned were manageable or symptoms of other underlying problems." The Advisor started to draw on a blank sheet of paper. "Let's create a list of all the things that get in the way of a typical day."

This was their list.

- Phone calls

- Computer problems

- Client management

- Supplier management

- Contractor management

- Staff performance

- Replying to emails

- Chasing payments by clients

- Questions on quotes

- Fixing mistakes by others (and us)

- Looking for lost paperwork

- Household chores

- Family 'crises'

Anna added, "I'm sure there are others that I haven't thought of."

"I'm sure you're right," agreed the Advisor, "but this is enough to start with. Let's see where you'd place these in a matrix of Importance vs Urgency. Something is important if it will make a long term difference to your business. Such as what we are doing today, but whether we scheduled the meeting today or next week, it would probably make little difference as long as this meeting was held. The results from such activities may not be immediately felt and may actually take a while to implement, but they are long lasting.

"Something is urgent if it can have a significant short term impact if is not addressed immediately. Usually it can be fixed reasonably quickly at a cost and some disruption, with a band aid solution, such as Luke getting a subcontractor to replace your employee, but there is no guarantee that it won't happen again. That is, the solution is usually not permanent. You are just getting yourself out of a hole. I call this fire fighting. So let's see where we'd put these and other issues you described earlier into this matrix."

There was some debate where some of the activities should go. "Weren't some client calls also important as well as urgent?" asked Luke.

"Not really," said the Advisor. "A single client's call rarely has a long term impact on the business, although if clients are all ringing up complaining about similar issues, that then becomes important. It may well be important to the individual client at that moment and it should be managed in a timely fashion, but I do acknowledge that for most clients, all calls are urgent and important.

Importance

Not Important/Urgent	Important/Urgent
Some email Some client calls Computer problems Lost paperwork Chasing client payment Questions on quotes Fixing mistakes Chasing Suppliers **GROUNDHOG DAY**	Family crises Staff Injury Fire Client Bankruptcy **LIGHTNING STRIKES**
Not Important/ Not Urgent	Important / Not Urgent
Most email Most phone calls Household chores **PROCRASTINATE NOW**	Business improvement meetings Staff performance **THE BUSINESS SWEET SPOT**

Urgency

Importance/Urgency Matrix

"This leads us to another point. The difference in perceived importance and urgency between the caller and the called, whether client, supplier or someone else. Often a call can be in response to poor organisation and management from either party. If you are that party, you need to deal with it. However, in most cases the call is in response to someone else's poor management. Too often we can get caught up with dealing with other people's crises. Most of these urgent calls by others can be managed with regular communication by you to the caller at times that suit you to prevent emergencies arising. Remember, they are calling you at a time that suits them. This may not be a time that suits you.

"Luke, you also asked about staff performance," reminded the Advisor. "It is a bit like client calls. If it's a single individual not doing his job properly, this may create an urgent situation as you experienced last week. However, if you keep having these problems with many of your staff, this issue becomes far more important, although on any given day you're managing it with additional supervision, so in that case it is not actually urgent today."

"It's possible to debate every item in this matrix, but I think we agree that this is a reasonable representation of reality," Anna interjected. "So how do we deal with this?"

Not Important/Not Urgent

"When you look at each quadrant, different responses are necessary. The Not Important/Not Urgent are the timewasters. They are things we often do to avoid the more difficult tasks. It's how we procrastinate. It's also work we do to 'save money'. An example of this is your household chores," said the Advisor. He asked Anna, "Could you hire a cleaner? Wouldn't the cost of a cleaner be far less than the value of your time? It might be a couple of extra hours you get back a week, but that could be time you spend on improving the business, or even quality time with Mark. Neither of these activities can be outsourced to anyone else."

"I could do that," agreed Anna.

"And Luke, I noticed the gardening equipment in your storage area. Do you do your own gardening?"

"Yes, I do."

"Could you hire someone else to do that?" asked the Advisor.

Luke nodded.

"As for the other items in that quadrant, Anna, could Sally screen your emails to determine which ones you need to attend to? Could you train her to recognise the timewasters? From time to time you might want to check the deleted emails just to ensure that nothing has been missed – as a kind of spot check."

"That makes a lot of sense," Anna agreed. "Those two changes alone could save me 3 hours per week."

"That's 1–2 days a month and we've just got started," the Advisor remarked encouragingly. "The time you spend in this quadrant is one of the main causes of your lack of time to achieve what you want in a day. You have to minimise the time you spend here. The message to take away is don't spend dollar time on penny jobs.

Not Important/Urgent

"The next quadrant is Not Important/Urgent. Work in this quadrant is usually evidence of a system failure, or an absence of a system in your business. Anna, you mentioned you lost some paperwork for a client last week which you eventually had to re-create from worksheets. While just a simple example, what this is telling us is that either your filing system is not adequate, or else it was not being followed. Which do you think it was?"

"I actually found the documents later. I put them in the wrong client folder. I remember I was in a hurry to pick up Mark from pre-school. How do you prevent such mistakes?" asked Anna.

"It's not easy, but one way is to ensure there is a back-up of all critical documents. The document could be scanned and stored digitally, before being placed in a folder. A little bit of extra work, but how often do you need to work with certain documents multiple times. And Luke, your supplier problem, what could you have done there?" inquired the Advisor.

After a second, Luke answered, "The supplier is normally reliable, but because this item was more difficult to source I could've identified alternate suppliers and had them on file just in case, rather than ringing around at the last minute. I'll make sure I make a file note of this alternate supplier for future reference."

"That's the idea." The Adviser appeared pleased with his answer. "Each of the tasks in this quadrant are symptoms of deeper problems with your business. I recommend you keep a problem log for any work that falls in this quadrant which should then be regularly reviewed to see what changes you can make to prevent a recurrence."

Luke thought for a moment. "What about questions on quotes? Obviously it's critical to our business that we win the job. I need to answer the questions or we could lose the job. How do we reduce that? Is it possible?"

"Luke, what I regularly see with questions on a quote, is that it's the same types of questions that are asked each time. So you need to make sure that your answers to these questions are clear in the quotes and in your explanation of the quote when you review it with them. Remember, your clients don't know as much about building as you do."

The Advisor continued. "Rather than reviewing the quote with them once, on such a complex and important sale as this, it may be worthwhile arranging a time for a second review after you go through it the first time. This is a way of addressing their legitimate concerns with a structured process that fits your schedule. The clients then won't feel they need to interrupt your day if they have a scheduled meeting with you.

"This quadrant is likely to soak up most of your time for little long term return. And not only your time, also the time of your staff – so this impacts significantly on your business and can easily cost a business 30% in lost productivity. This is where the fire fighting occurs, and you need to get out of the fire fighting business and stop the fires from starting in the first place. Putting systems in place to recover this time will transform your business. If you don't, it's Groundhog Day with the same problems happening over and over."

From Anna and Luke's expression, the Advisor could see he had made his point.

Important/Urgent

"Hopefully you don't have too many situations that occur in the Important/Urgent quadrant," the Advisor continued. "An example would be a family crisis. While Mark's illness was not a crisis, it was still both important and urgent. A bigger crisis would be if either of you were incapacitated. While many health issues can be avoided by living healthily, some can't. A more extreme example might be a lightning bolt destroying your house and office. This can be called the crisis sector, threatening the whole business almost immediately," the Advisor said quietly to emphasise the point.

"Now it's highly unlikely that such events would occur, but this is where planning is important. This could include insurance, and offsite backups – in case of fire. Also planning if one of you is unable to work for even a short time due to illness, or a disability which is far more possible."

"That's a good point," agreed Anna. "When I was unavailable last week, Luke didn't know where a lot of things were, and while Sally was very helpful, she couldn't find everything Luke needed, and he was unsure how I handled some things. A bigger issue would be if Luke was ill. While we have another supervisor, he can't do the quotes. We need to give some thought to that. I guess that is what you would call Important/ Not Urgent."

Important/Not Urgent

"That's right," the Advisor acknowledged. "The Important is often Not Urgent, but if you leave it too long, it becomes urgent. Work in this area keeps you out of the crisis quadrant and cures the symptoms you see in the Not Important/Urgent quadrant. It's the most valuable time you can spend on your business, and typically it's the area in which most business owners spend least time.

"This is where you develop the systems to prevent the recurrence of the problems you have to fix in the Groundhog quadrant. It's where you plan to mitigate against crises and how to improve the business. It's the Sweet Spot. It's where we are right now."

"How much time should we spend here?" asked Luke, pointing at the quadrant on the paper in front of them.

"In large business, executives spend most of their time in this quadrant because they have other people to manage everything else, doing the penny jobs. That's not possible in small business. Typically the owners will have some role in delivering the service. From what you've told me, you're only spending 10–20% of your time in the Sweet Spot. Luke is probably at the lower end of this range. Would you agree, Luke?" asked the Advisor.

"Possibly not even that most days," Luke replied, a little gloomily.

"Well, if we can eliminate the timewasters, and over time get out of the fire fighting business, you could increase the time in this quadrant to 30–50%. Is that enough? No, but it will be a great improvement, and what you'll find, as you increase the percentage of time in this zone, the easier it will be to increase it further.

"To finish off today," the Advisor continued, "I'd like you to keep a diary of what you're working on, identify which quadrant it falls in, and if it's not in the one you now know you have to be in, think of a way of eliminating that task in future. You do this by either delegating, outsourcing, creating systems to avoid the problem repetition, or stopping the activity altogether." As the Advisor was getting ready to leave he turned and said to both of them, "I also want you to finish the homework I gave you last time. No excuses."

"Right," said Anna. "That's a lot to think about, but I think I get it."

"These diary sheets you gave us will force us to think about how we spend our day, and we can compare at the end of each day to see who does best," Luke grinned.

Anna rolled her eyes.

Go to the Action Steps section for this Chapter now

Chapter 6

Seizing Back the Day

Over the next few weeks, Luke and Anna started to keep a diary of their time, but the patterns for each of them were quite different. Wherever possible, Anna stopped doing the penny jobs. She asked Sally to screen phone calls for her more thoroughly by carefully defining which ones should be put through straight away, such as messages from Mark's pre-school and from Luke, which ones she should take messages for, and which ones she could deal with herself.

As very few calls were put through to Anna straight away, this meant she was able to work uninterrupted most of the time. She chose the time to return calls when she wanted a break, or whether she would return them at all.

They worked out a similar system for emails, so rather than dealing with 30–50 emails a day, Anna only had to deal with a handful. She worked out with Sally how she should deal with the rest. Anna also hired someone to help with the household chores.

Unfortunately, Luke could not find ways to stop the interruptions. The clients all had his mobile number, as did numerous other people. He would regularly be asked to meet with clients on-site at short notice.

He was also fielding queries from on-site staff and suppliers and still had trouble finding the time to meet with potential clients or meeting architects who wanted to include him in their tenders.

When they met with the Advisor next, Anna declared, "The problem is that Luke is too obliging. The clients love him, because he can't say no. He will pop round to meet with them to discuss a problem on the way to the next appointment, and he ends up there for an hour and then he is very late to his next meeting. He's actually getting a reputation for being late, and I know it's not always his fault."

"In my defence," Luke countered, "if I don't deal with these things, we wouldn't have a business and some of them are important as well as urgent. I just can't see how I can delegate most of these issues."

"Luke, you have to take back control and not be at the beck and call of everyone else. Very few of these calls are urgent in the sense that they have to be dealt with that day. Would you agree?" asked the Advisor.

"Perhaps 20% need to be dealt with that day. Problems at one of our sites are usually the urgent ones. The clients always think their calls are urgent, but unless they impact on today's construction activity, which is rare, they aren't really," admitted Luke.

"Okay Luke, I am going to suggest something really radical. You don't answer your phone. We let the office manage your phone calls." Just as Luke was about to protest, the Advisor raised his hand. "I know what you're going to say, what about the 20% of the calls that are urgent, from your sites. Let's take this a step at a time.

"Firstly, let's focus on the non-urgent calls, the clients who want to meet with you. When you divert the calls to the office, the office will either set a time for you to call them back, or to meet with you at a time that fits with your schedule. This means that the office manages your schedule. This way the activities you planned at the start of each day, are able to be completed without interference.

"Secondly, rather than having the sites call you whenever they have the urge, you call them twice a day, once in the middle of the day to check progress and once at the end of the day to plan activities for the next day. These calls would be structured so that they are an effective use of your time and your supervisor's time. If you do this, for most issues your team will know that you will be available to them at the appointed time. How many calls from site would need to be made, apart from those times in a given day?" The Advisor was leaving no stone unturned.

"Well, very few," Luke conceded. "If we can plan activities twice a day, I can feel more comfortable about how things are going and there will be fewer surprises. But I still like to get out on-site regularly to make sure that what the guys are saying is actually happening."

"That is what I'd call an audit," explained the Advisor. "You don't have to be there all the time, but the fact that you might pop in at any time unannounced, and are there for certain critical events, means that your team feels they are being held to account.

"In addition, you should call into the office twice a day, when it suits you to see if there is anything truly urgent you need to deal with that day. This takes some trust. You have to trust Anna and Sally to manage these things for you."

"That was how it was when I asked Sally to start covering for me," Anna recalled."It was a trial and error at first, but really everything but Mark can wait an hour or two. So there were a few things that she didn't get quite right, but in reality, even for those things, my returning a call two hours later made no real difference. I found the experience a little scary at first, but now I find it liberating. In fact, when Sally was away at the beginning of this week, I realised how bad it used to be!"

"Alright," Luke agreed. "I'm willing to give it a go. It'll feel weird having my phone off. But what if there is a real emergency, like someone is injured on-site?"

"Could we get you a pager with a number only the office knows about?" Anna suggested.

Luke nodded. "That could work."

"These simple changes give you back control over your day without jeopardising your service or upsetting anyone. Remember, you'll make some mistakes in this new way of working, so you must be patient with each other as you work out the new rules," warned the Advisor. "You are on the same team, so at the end of each day for the first week or two, discuss what worked, and what didn't, and how you could change things for the next time."

"I'm excited by this new way of working, but I'm concerned that old habits might die hard," Anna said looking at Luke. "It all sounds good, almost too good to be true. It's one thing to agree in the office what will happen, but I know when Luke gets on-site, it'll be all too easy with the pressures he faces, to revert to fire fighting. While I'm not one of the boys, I have a pretty fair idea of what goes on."

Luke didn't say anything.

The Advisor then responded. "I never said this would be easy. There might actually be some backsliding, and we'll deal with that if and when it happens. At this stage it's important that you document the rules you develop to avoid misunderstandings. Whatever you do, try to avoid the blame game. No one is at fault while you are learning. Give it a go and see how it works."

"Mmmm. This should be an interesting couple of weeks if we don't kill each other first," Anna laughed as she nudged Luke. This time it was Luke who rolled his eyes.

Go to the Action Steps section for this Chapter now

Chapter 7

Emails to the Advisor

From Anna*

I want to let you know that I have resigned from Taylor Construction. I don't feel I can cope any more. With your help I thought we were getting somewhere but in truth the underlying problems are still there.

I feel I have to be constantly on Luke's back about his poor time management and communication skills. He is often late to site and meetings and I am often helping him to get ready and reminding him of the things he needs to take. He then gets angry with me for constantly hassling him.

Even though we agree on a course of action or policies and procedures he still goes his own way. When the boys see him changing things on the run I can't get them to follow our rules. They say: Well Luke says it's ok if we do it this way. What can I say to them then? I feel Luke is not supporting me and it makes it impossible for me to do my job.

*Author's Note: These emails are based on real emails sent to me by the wife and husband owners of a business to whom I was providing advice. They are used with their kind permission and have only been subject to minor editing. The passion in these emails is genuine.

I have been working hard to implement all of your ideas and I have been excited because I knew it felt right and it gave me the confidence that the decisions I was making were right. Everything we have worked on together has fallen into place and seems so clear to me but not to Luke.

Luke is very compassionate towards all clients and will do whatever he can to help solve any of their problems, including those not directly related to our project. This is a lovely attribute to have but the problem is that Luke doesn't understand when or how he should say "no". To be honest he is a bit of a soft touch.

I think Luke finds it easier to appease a client rather than stand his ground. He is very easily distracted from his work and will stop his work to help others. He doesn't understand where our work starts and finishes based on what we have agreed to provide service-wise, therefore others use him constantly to their advantage.

Luke is not conscious of time at all and he doesn't understand that "time is money". We should be registered as a "not for profit organisation". Luke does not intentionally go out of his way to undermine what I am trying so hard to accomplish but in reality he is the biggest thorn in my side.

From Luke's perspective he is confused about what he should say to clients because he worries about what I will say if he commits to things he shouldn't. He can't or doesn't know how to say "no" nicely to people. He is very unsupportive and rude to me when I feel that I give more than 100% to the business.

I am the one who is always worrying about returning client calls, delivering what we promise, looking after our staff, reminding Luke about the things he needs to do, trying to find better ways of doing things to deliver the best possible service to our clients, and contacting clients to ensure they are happy.

I live and breathe Taylor Construction. How can I do this when I feel that Luke is working in the opposite direction? I just can't see how we can continue to work like we are. If we want our own building business then Luke obviously needs to be involved. As we both can't work together because our work ethics are so different I think it best if I get a job or even start my own business in something different. If you can think of any alternative solutions or have any other suggestions I would be happy to hear them.

Regards Anna

From Luke

I understand that you have had some emails from Anna earlier. Apologies that you're caught in the crossfire. Probably most business consulting for businesses like ours have at some point, an aspect of domestic unrest.

I felt that I would like to present how I see things. Firstly, Anna paints a fairly unsavoury picture of me and that's okay because that's how she sees it. From my perspective, that is a large part of the problem. Everything is black and white, all the round pegs fit in the round holes and all the square pegs fit in the square holes.

Wouldn't it be great if that was always the case? But because of the type of business we are in, this isn't always how it pans out. Our planning and documentation systems are better, and our construction work output is improving.

When we undertake work on-site, we are faced with all sorts of challenges, some of which are generated by the site environment itself. When these occur, they come back to me. That's where the buck stops. Not with Anna. I have to deal with the clients, suppliers, sub-contractors, architects, and the council, to name a few. If the round peg doesn't quite fit in the designated round hole, someone is going to get hung out to dry and it will in every instance be me.

I do not receive any support from Anna dealing with the "issues" of the project. When a project 'blows out' it is a hunt for the guilty, which is always me. We do have hang-overs from past projects which will drag us back until they are completed and then we will be fully operating on our new strategy. That said, not everything is going to run like clockwork.

In the past few months, we have made a 90 degree direction change with how we operate and everyone is still coming to grips with this, and most of all, me.

The only person who understands all of what is in place is Anna because she eats sleeps and breathes it. She then becomes offended when we don't understand it or have difficulty implementing it.

I have come to the stage where I don't know what to do. If I make an appointment for a meeting, it will be at the wrong time. If I respond to an email regarding new work, I shouldn't have responded because it wasn't on the calendar. If I receive an email from an architect asking questions about a project and I forward it to Anna, I cop it because we shouldn't be doing that sort of work anyway.

I am at the point where I won't answer my phone because I would rather it going to the office and Anna deal with it. As an example, I had a call from an architect which fortunately for me, was diverted to the office.

Anna took the call and now we are doing this work which is a very small renovation and doesn't fit our project criteria. If I had taken the call, I would have been condemned for making any sort of commitment to the project, I would have been shown the criteria for an acceptable Taylor Construction project and if anything had gone wrong, I would have been given the smug "I told you so" routine.

We have a high level of staff turnover and I am not implying that it is because of Anna. The main issue is that no one can live up to her standards or expectations. Of the staff that have left, only one was worth having. He didn't like, as he put it, "being micro managed'. I must admit, that this is how I feel and I was somewhat relieved when Anna pulled the pin.

However, what Anna has done for the business in the past several months is nothing short of astounding but she wants to manage every single aspect of the business and everyone within it. There must be some happy medium?

Regards Luke

Chapter 8

Conversations

A Conversation with Anna

The phone rang. It was the Advisor. "Hi Anna, I know this is a stupid question, but how are you today?"

"Thank you for calling. I guess you saw my email. I just don't know what to do," Anna said quietly.

"Anna, I'm not calling to get you to change your mind about what you wrote. You obviously thought long and hard about it. All I want to do is find out what you want to do. Is that alright?" asked the Advisor.

"Yes," replied Anna.

"So let me ask you some questions. Firstly, what do you think will happen to Luke's business now that it's his alone?"

"Oh, I expect it to fold in the next year."

"You don't think Sally could step up and do what you have been doing?" queried the Advisor.

"No, I think she would leave. The only reason she has stayed is because I basically begged her to. She's still here because of me and in spite of Luke. She doesn't even know yet about my decision. She thinks I'm taking a break because of my pregnancy."

Anna paused, giving the Advisor time to ask, "And how do you think Luke would react if the business folded?"

"He'd be devastated. He has worked so hard. We both have, but Luke is far more attached to Taylor Construction than I am. He's its heart and soul. But I can't give any more." Anna started to sniff a little.

The Advisor was concerned. "If the business folded, what impact do you think it would have on your relationship?"

"I'm afraid that our relationship would be devastated, too," Anna responded. "I don't want that to happen. I still love Luke very much, but I can't see a way out. What choice do I have right now?"

"If there was a way that the problems you raised in your email could be fixed, would you change your mind about resigning?"

Of course," Anna replied, "but I can't see that happening with the way things are. I didn't want to resign, but I could see no other way to bring things to a head, and to get Luke to listen. Is there a way?"

"Possibly." After a pause, the Advisor continued, "If we can address some fundamental principles on how the business should be run and get an agreement between the two of you, it is possible. But both of you will have to compromise. I suspect that if we can fix this, pressures on other areas of your life together will reduce.

"I'll have a conversation with Luke. You know he sent me an email as well? "

"No, he didn't copy it to me like I did for mine to him," Anna said, "but I suppose I'm not surprised. What did he say?"

"While I won't go into detail," replied the Advisor, "I will say he was just as upset and frustrated as you are, and I think it is fair to say that he understands how big a loss you will be to the business. I'm not a marriage counsellor, but I do believe there is common ground. Let me explore that and we can see if it is possible to rebuild bridges."

"Thank you. I understand how this must be difficult for you, but I appreciate your efforts. I guess we pretend we can separate the business from the personal, but I can't," Anna conceded.

"You're right, it is extremely difficult, but you're not the first couple in business to go through this and you won't be the last. There is a pathway through this. I won't pretend it is easy, but it exists. The first step in this process is to get agreement that you both are prepared to take the journey."

"I am," sighed Anna. "I just hope Luke is."

A Conversation with Luke

"Hi Luke, have you got time for a chat about the future of your business?"

It was the Advisor, so Luke steadied himself. "I'm alone in the office right now, so yes I have time, although I'm not sure what more I can say."

"I'm not calling to tell you what to do, but rather to find out what you want to do. What I am going to do is to ask you a number of questions, is that alright?" The Advisor sounded friendly, rather than stern.

"Yes, it is."

"Firstly, tell me how you feel about Anna's decision," inquired the Advisor.

"Angry, hurt, let down, I don't know. Maybe a bit scared."

"How do you think your business will go without Anna's involvement?"

"I know I'm going to struggle, but if Sally can help out, I think I'll be able to make it," Luke replied, "but I'm going to have to work even harder now."

"Do you think Sally will be able to replace Anna?"

"No, probably not. It's not that she doesn't work hard, but Anna was just great in creating systems. She's done a huge amount taking your ideas and turning them into reality. I'm not sure how I can replace that, even with your help."

"So tell me what you think has gone wrong?" asked the Advisor.

"I don't know where to start. I suppose I feel that it doesn't seem to matter how well Anna organises things, the buck always has to stop with me. Only I can answer the questions from the architects, suppliers and clients."

The Advisor persisted. "How many of these problems that you're dealing with are fire fighting? For example, miscommunication with suppliers and clients? Last minute changes by the architects, or clarifications required on the plans? Redoing work that sub-contractors didn't do right the first time?"

Luke thought for a while. "Probably quite a lot, although often there will be surprises, particularly in renovation work on old buildings."

"These are two different issues," asserted the Advisor. "The first, the fire fighting can be reduced through better organisation and systems. The unexpected can be managed by incorporating risk when you provide a quote. In a renovation where it's not possible to inspect the condition of all areas before a job, you must allow for that risk. You can either make it implicit in your quote or explicit as a potential scope variation for the project. The trick then, is through your experience, to work out all the possible risks in a given type of job. Which comes back to systems again."

"What about staff issues?" asked Luke. "Anna doesn't understand what a good job on-site looks like."

"Perhaps not, but she does know if a task is going longer than you have budgeted, but only if your team are putting in their timesheets, and if there are client complaints about the state of the site – what I call hygiene issues. Can you see how she could manage the hygiene issues and you the technical ones?" The Advisor was certainly persistent!

"I can see that working," agreed Luke, cautiously, "but won't that lead to micromanagement of the staff? That's why some have left us."

"I think there would be an adjustment period while staff learn the new way of working. Micromanagement occurs when systems aren't in place or staff haven't been properly trained to follow the systems. After that it becomes more hands-off managing by reports."

"Yeah," said Luke still slightly sceptical, "but what about which jobs to bid on?"

"Don't you think that is another misunderstanding, this time on policy?" the Advisor continued to question Luke. "Look, it is not possible for Anna to get it right all the time any more than you will. The key is to have a process where you learn from the mistakes. Learning is more important than proving guilt. So how important is it to you that Anna come back into the business?"

"Honestly? If I think about what you've said, I know deep down this business won't survive without her. I'm not even sure we could survive as a couple. So the answer to your question is, I really need her to come back." Luke spoke frankly.

"And how prepared are you to give her the space to manage and even make mistakes?" persisted the Advisor.

"Do I have a choice? What we're doing now isn't working, so there really is no downside. Will you talk to Anna now to see what she wants to do?"

"No," the Advisor said firmly. "That's not my job, but it is yours. I can offer a process to manage these issues, but it will only work if you both are prepared to give it a try. I will wait for a call from you or Anna if you both agree that you are ready."

A conversation between Anna and Luke

When Mark was in bed, and they had cleared the dishes after dinner, Luke asked Anna to sit down so they could have a chat.

"I spoke to the Advisor today," he started, "I understand he's spoken to you as well." Anna nodded.

"Look Anna, I realise I can't do this without you. You've done so much to improve the business and I haven't really thanked you for what you have done."

"But you've been more than clear when you think I've messed up," Anna retorted, perhaps a little too sharply.

"I know. I have trouble admitting when I'm wrong, but I don't think you really understand how much pressure I feel. To make this work. To support our family," said Luke.

"I do understand Luke. It's why I've stuck with it so long. I know how hard you work and how tired you get, but the way we're going, all I could see was a train wreck waiting to happen. It's just not working. You can see that can't you?" Anna was struggling to contain her emotions.

Luke nodded. "But I think, deep down you want the business to work, that it supports all of us and keeps us together as a family. Do you want that?"

"I don't know, Luke. It'd be nice if it would work that way, but from where I sit at the moment, it all looks like a dream, or more accurately, a nightmare."

"Anna, what would it take to make the dream come true for both of us? What can I do? What can we do together?" Luke was almost pleading.

Anna said nothing for a while. "Luke, I don't want you to lose the business, but that is what I think will happen and I want to help you to make it a success. We can't run it the way we have in the past. The changes we need will probably be hard for us both, probably harder for you though."

Luke thought before responding. "I can see that. I also know I have to change because, well, the alternative is not an option, for the business, or for us as a family. Will you help me, Anna?"

"Yes, of course," said Anna. Luke started to hug, and kiss her. Anna drew back and said, "Not so fast. I'll call the Advisor in the morning," and gave Luke a peck on the cheek before she got up.

Chapter 9

Who's the Boss?

The Advisor detected some nervousness as he walked into their next meeting. There was politeness but the atmosphere was a little cool. "You have just been through a trial by fire, common to many couples Married to the Business." He smiled. "So let's begin. Today I want to talk about the roles you have in the business. I couldn't discuss that earlier, because you weren't ready. I think you are now."

Anna and Luke nodded.

"From what I know of you, Luke, you are never happier than when you're on-site working along side your staff, or sitting with a client going through their plans. The office side of the business is something which you are more than happy to let others manage."

"That's right," Luke agreed. "In fact, if I thought it was possible, I'd do less than I do right now. What I enjoy is the building process and the smiles I get from our clients when they get their keys. I know I'm not great at understanding Profit and Loss statements, Anna is much better at that than I am. I also know I have a responsibility to watch project costs."

"Luke, what you've described is the role of an Operations Manager. Responsible for project delivery, working with staff, suppliers and clients to produce what they are paying you for. Is that how you see yourself?" asked the Advisor.

"You know, that's exactly how I see my role. It's what I am good at," Luke agreed.

The Advisor now directed his attention to Anna. "And Anna, what about you. I believe that you're more interested in the overall performance of the business. Not just whether the projects are delivered on time and on budget, which is Luke's role, but also that the business makes enough money to pay all the creditors and staff, and there is enough left over for your family to have a comfortable lifestyle. That there are enough new enquiries that are turning into new business and that you have the capacity to handle all the work you get."

Anna nodded. "Also that the clients are happy, we get the jobs we want and avoid the jobs we don't. I also want to see the business become sustainable so it doesn't need such an effort from both of us, and to grow at a rate we can manage. I also dream that one day, we can hand over our business to our kids if they have an interest to run it like Bill's daughter did. That would be nice." She smiled.

"Anna, you have just described the role of a CEO. How do you feel about that?" the Advisor asked.

"Ha!" she laughed. "I'll need to start wearing braces and smoking cigars! I hadn't thought of it that way. Luke, what do you think?"

"I already thought you were the boss anyway," Luke laughed too.

The Advisor laughed with them. "Before we get ahead of ourselves, and Luke, you make Anna responsible for everything, you both have another role. Let me explain."

The Advisor started to draw a diagram on paper as he described what he had in mind. "We start with the ownership of your business. You are both owners 50/50. Every business has, or rather, should have a board where the owners sit. As from now, both of you sit on the board of Taylor Construction as directors. The board is responsible for everything that goes on in the business. The board determines the vision and develops strategy and policies for the business. It also reviews the performance of the business. I am just here as an advisor at your board meeting as I don't have a stake in Taylor Construction. So you are free to take my advice or not. But we are developing strategies now for your business.

The Advisor continued with his explanation. "The board does one other important thing. It appoints the CEO who is responsible for carrying out the wishes of the board, but reports back to the board. So if the board appoints Anna as CEO, she must still report back to the board where you both sit as equals. The CEO must report to the board on how the business as a whole is performing, but at the same time, the board also assesses the performance of the CEO. The board doesn't interfere in daily operations, but may at its meetings request changes in the management by the CEO based on how well the business does. Clearly with just the two of you in all the key roles, you have to be conscious of the hat you're wearing at any time because that dictates how you should act at that time. Is that clear?"

"So if I'm the CEO," started Anna cautiously "the board is my boss, so I'm my own boss with Luke as well? How does that work?"

"Consider a board for a listed company," explained the Advisor. "It'll have a mixture of owner representatives, executives and the non-executives who are not involved in the day-to-day operations. That's the role of executives. All these people, whatever their roles, work together to determine the correct strategy and policies for the business. The board agrees as a single entity what the correct course of action should be. Even though there may be differences in opinion, the board reaches a single final opinion as a result of negotiation and debate. It's then the CEO's role to implement the agreed board actions.

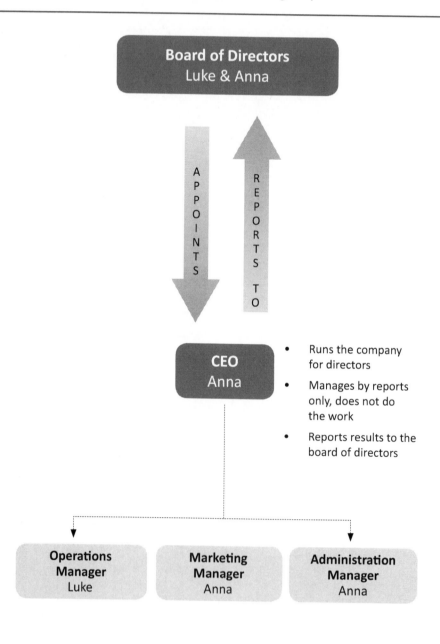

"The CEO doesn't have a right to unilaterally change the decision. If the CEO decides on reflection, the decision isn't in the best interests of the business; she still needs to go back to the board to convince them that a change in the decision is necessary, before implementing that action the way she wanted.

"Anna, if you take on the CEO role, you'll be taking the decisions that both you and Luke have agreed to at board level. You are the boss, just to the extent that you have the right to ask staff, including Luke, to assist you in implementing the decisions you both made at board level."

The Advisor turned to Luke. "I think you were concerned about a lack of control over operations. Do you have questions about this?"

"Actually, I really like this way of working together. Anna would be managing things in the way we have already agreed, and from time to time, monthly I think you suggested, I get to look at how well she has been managing the whole business. If there are significant issues, we can deal with them then. But what should I do if I see Anna is making a serious mistake?"

"As you do now, raise your concerns with her, but don't forget, she would have a different perspective to you. While you're focused primarily on the projects, she'll be looking at the overall finances and testing every decision against policy. Once Anna listens to your concerns, she should be able to refer back to the policies you had agreed at board level. The discussion should be at a policy level, not the single issue you are currently discussing."

The Advisor still had not finished. "Often there's a temptation to deal with decisions as 'special circumstances' requiring changes to policies on the go. That's where you are today. That means there's no consistency and you are continually taking an opportunistic approach, which is unsustainable. If you change your strategies and policies with frequent exceptions and exemptions, instead of having fixed goals to reach, you have to hit moving targets.

"Ultimately, you have to let the CEO make the final call. Not every call will be correct, but it should be rational. If the CEO makes a series of calls which can be seen to be incorrect in hindsight, there should be a review of decision making, strategy and policies at board level. Does that answer your question, Luke?"

"I think so," Luke replied. "I think it is much easier than debating everything and wasting time."

"I think we do waste a lot of time debating," agreed Anna. "What I often see is that the business becomes paralysed while we try to make up our minds. I often feel, almost any decision is better than no decision."

"I do have one other question," Luke said. "In the projects area, does Anna run that as well?'

The Advisor's response was definite. "No it doesn't. It just means you need to report on progress to her so she can see how the work is going compared with time and budget. It's her responsibility to manage the daily finances and to do forecasts for the financial year. As Operations Manager, you've a responsibility to ensure that work is to standard, as defined by your systems, and that your team are following your operational procedures. Anna wouldn't interfere with your operational management unless she could see serious impact on the rest of the business or she believed procedures weren't being followed. Her role is to ensure that Operations Management follows the agreed policies and achieves the outcomes for the business as set by the board."

"That makes sense," Luke agreed. "Our roles are quite clear, and we both are working under the direction of the board, which is us! A little confusing at first, but I can see it working. How about you Anna? Do you think that together we can make this work? Do you want to be CEO?"

Anna smiled. "I think this is what we have been missing and looking for. It's a structure that enables both of us to have our say with a process to resolve differences. I will take the CEO role, but I also need your support, Luke, because I know there'll be mistakes. I can't do it on my own."

Luke confirmed his agreement. "I think these rules and structures will mean I can give you support and know that things will be done, not just the way I want them to be done, but the way we both agree on. I also know there is a process I can follow without confrontation if I think things are not happening the way they should."

"I feel a lot more comfortable now," said Anna. "It all seems to start with a board meeting." Anna turned to the Advisor. "How do we manage that?"

"I will send you an agenda," answered the Advisor. "In the meantime, I want you to think about what you want from your business." With that, he stood, collected his papers and left after saying good bye.

Go to the Action Steps section for this Chapter now

Chapter 10

What Do We Want?

Their advisor had informed them that this must be their own vision, not his. While he could help them formalise it, they must make the first attempt themselves.

"What DO we want?" asked Luke. Mark had just been settled for the night and Anna and Luke were sitting at their kitchen table having a coffee.

"For the business or us?" wondered Anna.

"It really comes down to the same thing I guess," Luke said, taking a sip from his mug. "I realise now this business only exists to support our family. Although I really enjoy being out on-site, and working with my team, I could just as easily have got that satisfaction working for Bill and leave all the headaches of running a business to him."

"But even when you worked for Bill you had your bad days," Anna remarked. "Things you couldn't control. The way Bill liked doing things was not always the way you wanted to do them. I think there's more to our business than just supporting the family. It's something we've created together. I'm quite proud of what we've achieved, even with its problems. It's ours – for better or worse we are married to the business," she laughed.

You're right! After what we both know now, I think it'd be hard for us to work for anyone else again. We'd see all the flaws – and wouldn't shut up about them. We're probably unemployable now! I think if we got jobs we'd be taking a step backwards."

Anna took out two pieces of paper and gave one to Luke. "Why don't we write down some things we want from the business."

Over the next 10 minutes, they each wrote out their own lists of what they wanted. When they compared them, they noticed most items were the same, even if worded differently. Although each had a few unique things they wanted, neither objected to the additional items on each others list.

Anna merged the lists to come up with a single list.

- Profitable

- Sustainable

- Manageable Growth

- Enjoyable

- Family Friendly work environment for ourselves and our staff

- Legacy for our children

- Team Taylor comes before individual Taylors

- Happy clients who tell all their friends about Taylor's

- Happy staff who enjoy working at Taylor's

- Reputation for quality

- Others want to deal with us because the way we work

- Minimise stress

- Work/Life balance for the Taylor Team

They were pleased with this combined list. The next step, was to turn these wants into a series of statements about the business. Working over the course on an hour, and after many re-writes, they had something upon which they both agreed:

Vision for Taylor Construction

Taylor Construction has a reputation as an upmarket home builder with a focus on client satisfaction providing its services within a half hour drive of its offices. As a result of this reputation, most of its business comes from referrals. It is a well managed business that does not require the Taylor family to be present at all times for it to operate smoothly. Its growth is steady, without compromising its ability to deliver the results that its clients demand. The business is profitable and always able to pay their staff and creditors, and always able to provide a comfortable standard of living for the Taylor family. It will meet their work/life balance needs and will have in place processes to minimise the stress of running the business.

As a family business Taylor's will ensure that it meets the needs not only of the lifestyle of the Taylor family, but wherever possible the family needs of our employees. Good management of the business and enjoyable work conditions will ensure low staff turnover.

The long term vision for the business is to be able pass management of the business to the next generation of Taylors once they have the experience and confidence to operate it themselves, and if they have that desire themselves.

Luke looked at Anna and smiled. "All we have to do is to turn our vision into reality. How hard can that be?"

Go to the Action Steps section for this Chapter now

Chapter 11

A Helicopter View

Agenda for the Board Meeting for Taylor Construction

1. Review Actions from Last Meeting

2. Performance Review of Period

   2.1 Highlights of period – contribution to goals

   2.2 Current obstacles to plan achievement

   2.3 Key Performance Indicator Review

   2.4 Financial Report

   2.5 Marketing Report

   2.6 Business Operations Report

   2.7 Staff Performance Report

3. New Opportunities Review

4. Any Other Business

5. Action Plan

"Today we run our meeting according to this Agenda," the Advisor announced passing copies of the Agenda to Anna and Luke. "I'll act as Chairman today, and for the next few meetings, but I would like one of you to take over when we get to a more routine stage. I suggest Luke should be the chair at that time, because I don't believe the CEO should also be the chair as the CEO is reporting to the board. "This may all may appear rather formal, but having a structure is a way of managing differences and ensuring that all important issues are addressed. It also can help avoid getting bogged down in detail. Anyone can add items to the agenda, but it should be done ahead of time so that the preparation can be completed before the meeting. This way all the background information is available to discuss and resolve the issue. Are there any questions?"

Anna started to raise her hand, and then laughed. "This is all a bit serious, but of course it is. I just wondered why you waited until now to create the board like this. Why not at our first meeting?"

"Because you weren't ready," the Advisor said. "When we first met, your business was in serious trouble. It would have been like a doctor saying to a patient who was gushing blood from a deep wound, 'You know I think really you need to lose some weight, let's put you on a diet first.' We first had to bring things into some semblance of control. And change as radical as we have just made required a major shift in thinking from you both. It took a crisis to achieve that. As Churchill once said, 'Never let a good crisis go to waste.' The crisis made you both open to different ways of thinking, as the current ways were obviously not working."

"I'm sure I would have shown you the door if you suggested this on our first meeting," Luke agreed. "But now I really think this is the answer for us."

"This is not a silver bullet," cautioned the Advisor. "There will no doubt be other crises. The trick is not to have the same crisis twice, and to use this process to identify possible future problems so most crises can be avoided.

1. Review Actions

"Getting back to our Agenda. The first item is to review the homework or actions from the last meeting. The most important of these was the Vision for Taylor Construction. Let's discuss this now." The Advisor waited for Luke or Anna to respond.

"We are quite pleased about what we wrote together, but I'm a bit concerned that it needs a bit more polish. What do you think?" Anna asked.

"I wouldn't spend too much time in polishing, as you describe it. As a first attempt, it's fine, and it's in your own words, not those of some consultant, so you understand what they mean. In any event, you will probably want to make changes as we implement this vision, so let's not spend time polishing it any further at this time," the Advisor answered.

"How often should we be changing our vision?" asked Luke.

"You should have a good hard look at it once a year to make sure it is still relevant to your circumstances, but I strongly discourage frequent changes, because your vision just becomes a whim that is never realised. The next step is to understand what the strategic implications are from your vision. From this we can create an implementation plan."

The Advisor pulled out another sheet of paper and started to deconstruct the vision statement into strategy summaries checking with the Taylor's whether they agreed with each statement.

Marketing Strategy

Taylor Construction will build a reputation as a reliable upmarket home builder in the eastern part of the city with attention to client satisfaction which will generate referrals for the business from clients and their architects. Growth will be managed so that there is no damage to their reputation.

Operating Strategy

Taylor Construction will have systems in place to ensure that projects run smoothly, that clients are satisfied with the service provided and that the business does not depend on the Taylor's presence every day. It will have staff policies to ensure that it is a family friendly business and that employees enjoy working at Taylor's resulting in high productivity and low staff turnover.

Business Strategy

Good management of the business will underpin its success. Manageable growth targets would be set and achieved with good planning and implementation processes. Management reports will enable the business to function without the Taylor's continuous presence.

Profit objectives will be set to enable the Taylor family to receive a good return for their risk and efforts and ensure all liabilities are paid when due. This will be achieved through careful cash flow management.

Family Strategy

A balance between business growth and family lifestyle will be achieved by setting growth targets consistent with this objective and ensuring that their business management systems are robust enough to allow time away from the business for either Anna or Luke or both as it is needed.

The long term strategy is to build a business in which their children, can work and in time, if they desire, run themselves when Anna and Luke wish to step out of operations.

When they had finished, the Advisor looked at both of them and explained, "At the moment these are still just words, but in each statement there are a number of strategies that need to be developed to make all this happen. The first is your Family Strategy. Here are some questions you need to answer. I will write them down so that you can answer them together."

The Advisor began his list of questions.

• What income do you both need to live comfortably now?

• What income would you like to have in five year's time?

• How many hours a week would you each want to work now, and in five years?

• How will you manage your business alongside your family duties? What time constraints does that place upon you both?

• What regular time off do you both want now, and in five years?

The Advisor continued. "Using the technique we covered in our first meeting and your answers to these questions, you can now create Profit and Loss statements for 12 months and five years from now and set your profit objective.

"Let's now talk about your Business Management System. While you already have some parts of it in place, we need a plan to make it cover the whole of your business. This is what will enable you to have a business that runs without you. Now I warn you, this will take time to build, a reasonable timeframe might be a year, but even then, it won't be finished. It never is!

This is what a business Management System looks like." The Advisor pulled out yet another sheet of paper from his briefcase.

"You can see the components of the Business Management System, which include your vision and goals, your key business areas, the procedures in each area, the description of the roles for each position and the people undertaking those roles. It also includes performance benchmarks for each role, describing what a good job looks like. Here are the key business areas."

The Advisor reached for another sheet, with the Key Business Areas listed on it.

- Strategic Business Development

- Management and Reporting Systems

- People

- Financial

- Marketing

- Administration

- Legal

- Information Technology

- Operations

- Risk Management

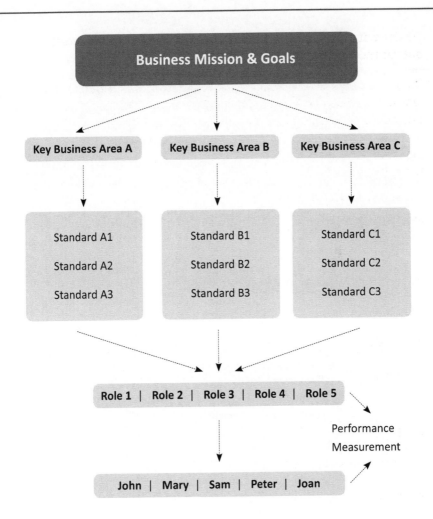

BUSINESS SYSTEM SCHEMATIC

"In each of these areas, you may have dozens of tasks and procedures, and particularly in your operations area, Luke, probably hundreds. It will take time to put all this in place, so you must prioritise depending on the impact each system might have on your business. The first step is to identify all the systems you need to create and then make a plan to write the procedures, according to your prioritisation. A very important part of any procedure is some kind of reporting so you know it has been done correctly. It might be something as simple as a checklist signed off by the person performing task. Here is a list of some of the systems in each of the key business areas I was speaking about." The Advisor presented them with more documents listing dozens of sample systems required for any business.

> See the Resource page for access details for this document.

"Some of the key systems that are referred to in your Vision statement and in the Strategy Summary, which will be critical to your success, are:
- Customer Service Procedures
- Financial Reporting Systems
- Project Cost and Time Reporting Systems
- Project Management Systems
- Reputation Management Systems
- Referral Systems

"These should be systems that you prioritise. Go through the complete list and determine which ones you want to have in place in the next 30, 90 and 180 days and who will be responsible for putting them in place. This is something that you should report on each month."

"I'll have a plan for the implementation of our Business Management System for our next board meeting," Anna noted. "What's next on the Agenda?'

2. Performance Review

"The next item is a performance report for the last month. However as this is the first time we have done this, I'd just like to spend this time discussing what the performance report should look like. The first part of this report is to list highlights for the business. It might be winning a big contract or that all productivity goals have been met. This might seem a little artificial when it's just the two of you, but it's too easy to focus on what went badly. There's nothing wrong with giving yourselves a pat on the back. By having this as a formal part of your reporting, it can assist you in maintaining morale, even in difficult times."

"Well, last month," Luke began, "we actually finished one project ahead of time, which hasn't happened for quite a while."

"And I was able pay off all our creditors this month and there was enough money left over, which we can now spend on redecorating our house. That's something we've talked about for some time," added Anna. "I also put a bit extra into the pay for the boys as a thank you."

"That's great," said the Advisor. "What I'd suggest is you each look for two or three things that went well in your areas of responsibility. It's also something you should share with your staff so they have a feeling that they are working in a business that can provide for them and of which they can be proud.

"The next part of the report are obstacles to achieving your plan. This could be supplier problems or staff issues, or even a family illness. It's difficult to keep apart the personal from the business side, but you must be up front when it is affecting your business, after all a lot of people are depending on the business now."

"Well, I haven't made a list, but one of my bug bears at the moment is getting the boys to fill in their timesheets each week so we can track project costs properly. I even find it hard getting them from Luke," Anna declared, looking at Luke.

"I do tell them to fill them out," Luke protested, "and I do my best as well, but we do get busy on-site."

"This is the time when you look for resolution of these issues. Do you have a system for this?" The Advisor looked from one to the other.

"I have created timesheets for the boys to fill out," Anna replied. "It should only take them a few minutes a day, but they tend to leave it to the end of the week. Luke just needs to insist on them doing it each day as part of the pack up routine before they leave."

"Luke, do you agree this information is important to manage your projects properly?" the Advisor asked.

"Yes, I know it is important, and it shouldn't take long. I will start insisting they do it before they go home," agreed Luke.

"This is an example of how to address issues that may be affecting either of you in business in a non-confrontational way. Recognising that this is important to the business, that you had agreed to take certain action, and then looking at ways of making it easier to comply. You're both on the same team, remember. It's in both your interests to solve the problem. Look for solutions, not blame.

"Let's look at the next Agenda item," continued the Advisor. "The Key Performance Indicator (KPI) report. This is a single page summary of all the other reports. It's like the dashboard for your business where you can quickly identify where the major areas of focus should be. The subsequent reports are the next level of detail for your dashboard. We can decide what the gauges on your dashboard should be after we complete the other reports.

"The first of these is a review of your financials. It is important that you can produce your financial reports as close to the end of the month as possible. The longer you leave them, the less useful they are. It starts with your Profit and Loss statement and your cash flow forecast. Both of these reports should be compared against your budget. There are many other measures that are useful. Here's a list of some other measures you should consider in your financial report." The Advisor tabled another document listing numerous other financial measures.

See the Resource page for access details for this document.

"Not all of these will be applicable to your business, but many will be. All this information should be easily extractable from your accounting software."

"I think this will be very useful, and I'll be able to see very quickly how the business is doing month to month," Anna responded, reading through the material.

Luke looked a little concerned. "Anna, you are going to have to show me how I should read this. I can see it's something I must understand, but I'll need your help."

"Luke, it will give you context for all the daily decisions that Anna may make," explained the Advisor. "It'll also reduce the conflicts as you are both looking at the same dashboard. The first item on your dashboard will probably be your cash position. Satisfying yourselves that you have enough money in the bank to operate the business is vital before looking at the rest of your business. As I like to say, Cash is King." The Advisor paused, allowing Luke time to consider this before he continued.

"Our next priority is to look to the future of your business, which is your marketing. This starts with looking at your enquiries, and then examining how they are progressing through your sales pipeline, to the point where you complete a sale. Now in a business like yours, you don't need a lot of sales to be sustainable, given that one of your projects might take six months to complete. In your case, you may look at these statistics over the last quarter rather than the last month, but other types of businesses would have much shorter time frames. Supermarkets are at the other extreme. They look at sales on an hourly basis!

"Here are some suggested measures for your marketing to see how effective it has been." The Advisor dug out another sheet of measures for them both.

See the Resource page for access details for this document.

"The enquiries should be broken up by source, so you can see the effectiveness of your marketing campaigns. You can use these reports to forecast your business. A healthy flow of enquiries, which you know from history that you can effectively convert to sales, indicates a positive future. A change of enquiry rate for the worse is a leading indicator of problems ahead. Enquiries and sales are the lifeblood of any business."

"To be honest, we haven't really been tracking this systematically," Anna admitted. "It has all been a bit ad hoc. We get the enquiries and fit them in with our other activities, but this gives them the prominence they deserve. Doing it this way makes us focus on improving our sales systems."

"While you, Anna, are largely responsible for these reports, the Operations reports are very much Luke's responsibility, even though you and Sally may be compiling the figures. Here you should be looking at how the projects have been proceeding against plan and your initial quotation. Are they on track? Are they falling behind? If they are falling behind, it's important to identify that fact as early in the project as possible so you can take corrective action before you blow your budget. Here are some measures you might want to consider when looking at operational performance." Again, the Advisor gave them some more measures, this time operational. "Of course these are general, but you can see how they can be adapted to your business."

See the Resource page for access details for this document.

"I think these will be quite useful. I want to be better able to track our on-site productivity. More forms I guess." Luke smiled wryly.

"Finally you should have a report on your staff. You have a small staff, so statistics are not so useful, but this is a place where you can raise staff issues. It could be an individual, if there was a performance problem with a staff member, or it could be more general such as training or an incentive program."

"That reminds me," Anna interrupted. "We need to do the summer leave roster."

"Anna, that's important, but is fairly detailed, not for a board discussion, except perhaps on how many people you need to cover that period, and when you hope to take leave. So this is probably more an action item for you to follow-up outside this meeting. You may have a short meeting outside the board to finalise it. It's too easy to try and use this time to solve problems like this which are best solved separately, as they typically require a lot of information you don't have, such as in this case, who wants to take leave when."

"I can see that," said Anna. "We just need to be prepared to pick each other up when we try to solve such detailed problems in the board meeting."

3. New Opportunities

"Yes, it's the only time in a month when you work on the business in this way, and you mustn't use that time to work on operational issues," the Advisor continued. "The next stage in the meeting is New Opportunities. This could be anything from a new piece of expensive equipment that Luke believes will increase productivity to a new marketing opportunity, such as a website upgrade you might want to consider together because of the amount and nature of the expenditure. It might also include considering a different type of client, such as property developers, and whether that is something the business wants to pursue.

"Few of these major decisions are urgent, and can be put on hold to the next board meeting where they can be considered in a naturally strategic environment, rather than squeezed between operational matters during the month. The person bringing the opportunity to the board needs to have prepared the background information which will be needed for a decision to be taken and be able to say how this will assist goal achievement and how it is consistent with your strategy."

"Does that mean we can't raise opportunities outside our current strategy?" asked Luke.

"Not at all," the Advisor replied, "but you must also in that case be prepared to have a discussion on why the strategy should be changed. This puts a brake on the temptation to become fashion followers. It becomes a considered decision. Working for property developers, I'd suggest, would be a major change for you with significant implications to your business, both good and bad."

"I want to stay clear of those guys, they're mostly cowboys and slow payers, but I take your point," Luke agreed.

4. Other Business

"I think the rest is self explanatory," the Advisor continued. "You should also have much shorter meetings each week, which should probably include at least some of your staff to plan your operations and make sure you're making progress towards your monthly goals. These are great ways to find out what is happening in your business. It also tends to reduce interruptions, because people know they can raise non-urgent matters regularly at that time."

"Wow, that's quite an agenda. Are we done now?" Anna asked looking at her notes.

"Not quite," replied the Advisor. "We need to agree on the action items for the next month."

"I have those already written down," Anna reported putting the action items in front of Luke and the Advisor. These were Anna's notes.

5. Action items for next board meeting

1. Answer questions on family goals (Luke and Anna)

2. Set profit objectives for now and in 5 years (Anna)

3. Identify the systems required for each Key Business Area – Operations (Luke) the rest (Anna) and prioritise

4. Develop the reports and the KPI's we will use for our financials and marketing (Anna), operations (Luke) and staff (both)

5. Produce these reports for the next board meeting

6. Start holding weekly meetings

"That's great," said the Advisor. "We can conclude the meeting. Next board meeting, we will follow the agenda the way it was presented today, and the first item on that agenda will be those actions."
"No pressure then," laughed Luke.

Go to the Action Steps section for this Chapter now

Chapter 12

A Good Month

Anna and Luke felt energised. They knew exactly what to do, and they did it. They spent time with their staff and explained what they were planning and they were also excited. It was good to be associated with a business that knew where it was headed and recognised the importance of family. Even the young single guys in Luke's team could see the value of this.

Anna and Luke held their first weekly meeting, inviting Sally, and Luke's supervisor, Jack. Anna started off by presenting the goals for the week, and listening to the concerns of Sally and Jack. Anna and Luke were unaware of a number of the issues they raised, but after discussion, priorities were adjusted and their concerns could be met. Jack and Luke agreed to hold similar meetings with the on-site teams to explain the plans as it affected them and ensure that their concerns were addressed as well.

While issues certainly occurred during the month, they were able to be handled with only minor impact on the business goals. In fact, a number of problems that could have become serious were raised by staff ahead of time and were able to be managed.

One example of this was that Sally noted that a contract with a new client was on an old form which provided lesser protection for the business. Anna was able to speak to the client and persuade them to come into the office and re-sign the new contract. Sally ensured that all the old forms were destroyed and the digital version of the old form was archived. Anna also created a system to ensure that any new versions of documents properly replaced older versions to prevent such problems in the future.

On-site, one of Jack's team noted that a plumbing contractor was not following the plans that the team had reviewed together earlier that week and alerted Jack to the problem after the contractor disputed the error. Jack was able to intervene, after a 'frank exchange of views', and prevent an expensive mistake. Jack resolved to spend more time with contractors to ensure that they understood what they needed to do before they started.

Anna was pleased how the month progressed, and Luke seemed quite content in his new role within the business. There was a lot less time fire fighting, with more fires being prevented before they started. This allowed much more time to spend on achieving their goals and for both of them to work on the action list from their board meeting.

One evening Luke and Anna sat together and answered the questions on the Family Goals. It was an enjoyable activity for both, imagining a future together. The only downside from this was it meant Anna now had to turn these goals into financial forecasts, but following the process provided by the Advisor, she was able complete that task.

Systems Planning

While putting together a list of the non-operational business systems was fairly straight forward for Anna, for Luke it was a major exercise. Anna could quickly see where the gaps were, and came up with some extra systems that weren't on the Advisor's list.

Luke decided he would break his task into stages of the building process, starting from estimation and quoting, excavation, foundations, all the way to Lock-up and handover. He realised that this would take some time, so he planned to go through the procedures as they occurred in his current projects. As he did this, he regularly consulted with Jack, who provided some great advice on some of the areas that he saw were missing.

Both Anna and Luke highlighted urgent systems that should be developed straight away, and identified those that could wait until either next month, or later in the year.

While Anna was able to complete this task, they both agreed that Luke should have more time and together they developed a plan over the next six months that he would follow.

Preparing Reports

A much bigger job for Anna was creating the reports for the next board meeting. She started by taking each business area, and using the suggestions from the Advisor, worked out the information she wanted to see. She even drew a mock-up of what the report should look like.

For each measure that she wanted in the report, she had to determine where the data would come from. For the Financial Report, almost all could come from their accounting software, although there were a couple of measures that would have to be calculated from the numbers the software produced. She also noted that she would have to change the chart of accounts to provide more detail in the future, but there were no serious problems, except it normally took 3 weeks to produce the accounts after the end of the month.

Anna sat with Sally to see how all this could be done. Part of the problem was they were waiting to the end of the month to commence entering the data into the software, and then finding that some of the paperwork was missing. They agreed to change things so that the accounts would be updated on a weekly basis, which meant at the end of the month it was just the last week that needed to be entered.

When Anna started on the Marketing Report, she realised that they were not currently collecting all the data, especially at the early stages of their marketing funnel before the first face-to-face appointment with a new client. She had asked the Advisor if there was a simple way of doing this, and he mentioned Client Relationship Management (CRM) software that is designed for this purpose, but as they only received a handful of enquiries each month, it could be handled just as well in a spreadsheet for now. Anna asked Sally to create spreadsheets to collect the information needed for the marketing report.

Operations, again was the headache. She sat with Luke to design reports for his area. Once Luke saw the potential for these reports he became quite enthused. Perhaps too enthusiastic, as it became evident that his desire for information was more than their ability to supply it. "Let's not be too ambitious," Anna cautioned. "At the moment you're really getting nothing until well after month's end. I know you feel you are operating blindly, but let's walk before we run."

Luke agreed, so they negotiated a simpler report. "Luke, you realise, while Sally and I can put this information together, it all has to come from you and team. That means more forms!"

"I know," Luke nodded, "but I can see the value of the information. If we can collect the information in real time, rather than trawling over invoices and payslips at the end of the month, it shouldn't be a real burden. For example, we can start recording expenditure with suppliers at the time of ordering with a job code and enter it into our accounting software each week."

"It will take a little time to set up, but at least we know what we want now," agreed Anna.

The last reporting area was staff performance. Having looked at the Advisor's list, they realised they had few systems in this area. Anna undertook to put these systems in place over the next six months, and as they only had a small number of employees, they would just discus the issues such as performance problems or hiring new staff as they arose.

They both felt that there really weren't any significant problems at this stage with everyone seeming to like the new way of operating.

"Well, I think we'll be ready for the board meeting in ten days," Anna observed.

"I think I can also put together, even if by hand, a useful Operations Report," added Luke, "although it won't be as good as I would like, but I won't let the perfect be the enemy of the good. For the first time, I'm looking forward to this Board Meeting."

Go to the Action Steps section for this Chapter now

Chapter 13

The CEO Reports

"Let's start with a review of the actions from last month's meeting," said the Advisor.

1.   Review Actions

"The first action was to write out our family goals based on the questions you provided. Here are answers." Anna placed a sheet on the table.

1.   *What income do you both need to live comfortably now?*
     We are seeking a combined income of $150,000 next financial year in addition to a net profit of 10% of turnover, which may be at least partly re-invested in the business. Last year we cleared $80,000 with no net profit or allowance for depreciation.

2.   *What income would you like to have in five years time?*
     We are seeking a combined income of $300,000 in addition to a net profit of 10% of turnover which may be at least partly re-invested in the business.

3.   *How many hours a week would you each want to work now and in five years?*

At the moment Luke works 60 hours per week and Anna works 40 hours. This year we want this to reduce to 45 hours for Luke and 30 hours for Anna. In five years we would like the hours to be 35 for Luke and 30 for Anna.

4. *How will you manage your business alongside your family duties? What time constraints does that place upon you both?*
At the moment, Anna's hours are spread over the time Mark is at pre-school and some evenings. Mark's grandparents also look after him several times a week and Luke's niece does some child minding. When the baby is born, Anna will take a month off. We have arranged someone to come in and help Sally. When Anna returns to work, her mother has offered to look after the baby one day a week and Luke's mother on another day. Anna believes with Sally's support and the part-time support of another assistant that she will be able manage 30 hours a week.

5. *What regular time off do you both want now and in five years?*
We would like to be able to take a month off every year, which will probably be in summer when we are not so busy. In five years we would like to go on a two month vacation in Italy to visit with Anna's relatives who are still living there. Both children should be old enough to enjoy the holiday as well.

The Advisor nodded approvingly. "Have you prepared new profit forecasts?"

"Yes," said Anna as she added another sheet to the table.

"What are your assumptions other than your increased wages and net profit?" asked the Advisor.

"I've assumed that we do seven houses next year, we increase our efficiency by another 5% and Luke spends less time on-site," Anna noted. "In five years we will have doubled the size of the business, Luke won't be on the tools at all and we'll be leasing an office away from our home to cater for extra staff. There are also other cost consequences I've included in the forecast."

Taylor Construction Profit & Loss		
	Next Year	In 5 Years
Sales	**2,500,000**	**4,600,000**
Labour	479,000	895,000
Subcontractors	341,000	640,000
Materials	907,000	1,680,000
Gross Profit	**773,000**	**1,385,000**
Overheads		
Advertising	10,000	20,000
Dues & Fees	35,000	35,000
Equipment Costs	10,000	15,000
Insurances	30,000	40,000
Labour	259,050	559,050
Office Expenses	22,000	40,000
Telephones and IT	6,000	10,000
Vehicle Costs	30,000	40,000
Vehicle Leases	70,000	85,000
Other Expenses	20,000	30,000
Total Overheads	**492,050**	**874,050**
Depreciation	30,000	40,000
Net Profit	**250,950**	**470,950**

"You realise that you've just presented an executive summary of a business plan to me?" smiled the Advisor.

"If you include my documentation of this forecast, I could claim it's not just a summary, but a complete plan," said Anna. "For example, I considered what our marketing plan should be and put those costs into the budget, and how staff should change as we grew."

"That's good work, Anna," the Advisor said. "How have you gone with the systems?"

"I've identified missing systems for the non-operational areas of our business and have a plan to put these in place over the next six months. I will report on progress on that plan over the coming months at board level," Anna replied.

"My job in this area is massive, and I have broken it into project stages," added Luke. "We'll complete the whole cycle over the next six months, identifying all the systems, putting in place those which are urgent immediately, and prioritizing the rest. I'll also report my progress on a monthly basis."

"Very good," the Advisor commented. "We can leave the reporting on the remaining actions until the relevant section if you like."

"That would be fine," Anna agreed. "Also we've started the weekly meetings, which have been a great success."

2.1 Highlights from Previous Month

"Right, the next item on the Agenda is the highlights of the month. Who would like to start?" asked the Advisor.

"I will," answered Luke. "The on-site team members are really pleased about the weekly briefings. The feedback has been very good. They feel like their ideas and opinions are valued, which they are, but having a formal process like this makes them really feel appreciated. Another highlight was at the end of the month when we brought the teams together for a bar-b-que as a way of thanking them for their great work. They don't get together much as a group and we included Sally and Anna as well. Finally, one of the projects we were working on was well over budget because of many problems. I'm now forecasting that we will achieve budget, thanks to some better planning and some work practices changes that allows us to multi-task some parts of the job."

"On the general business side," Anna continued, "we picked up two new clients which means we have work scheduled for the next six months. This is the second month in a row that our creditors are up to date, which hasn't happened for a long time, and we're now issuing invoices the day the payment milestones are reached rather than a week or two later. This has improved our cash flow greatly. We were also able to pay ourselves our target amount from our Family Goals and still have enough in the bank to cover next month's creditors and payroll."

2.2 Current Obstacles

"That's a great report," acknowledged the Advisor. "What issues are you currently facing?"

"It's mainly time," replied Anna. "We worked a lot of extra hours to get this done. I'm not complaining, but I can't keep up this pace with my current condition," patting her stomach with a growing bulge inside. "I get quite tired now."

"I think the systems are definitely helping us," noted Luke. "I'm sure next month will be easier, and the months after that. I'm thinking that we could bring the additional assistance for Anna forward by a few months. What do you think, Anna?"

"I think we can afford it and I certainly can do with the help right now. Let's get her in next month. I'm also concerned about all the work Luke is doing. He's getting much more done now, but is still putting in too many hours."

"I know a lot of the work you do, Luke, is highly technical, but what parts could you give to others with sufficient experience?" asked the Advisor.

"Putting together quotes based on the plans I receive can be quite a lengthy process. I am quoting on less now and our success rate last quarter, 2 out of 3, is pretty good. The one I lost wasn't one I really wanted to bid on. It was more a favour for an architect. So I could be more choosy. I could also use an estimator, which will reduce my time substantially. I'll give some thought to that."

"Can you also come up with better criteria on what jobs you will quote on in the future? Perhaps you could review the jobs you won and lost over the last year," suggested the Advisor.

"I think we can do that together," Anna answered. Then looking at Luke, she continued, "The other problem we have at the moment is getting a couple of the boys to complete timesheets when they should, but we are working on that with a little carrot and stick approach, and I believe that this will sort itself out. I think those are the key problems we are facing at the moment."

2.3 Key Performance Indicator Review

"Moving to the next item on the Agenda. Do you have a KPI dashboard for the business to show me?" asked the Advisor.

Again Anna placed another sheet in front of the Advisor.

The Advisor asked both, "Do you think if you were away from the business and received a single page with the highlights, issues and this dashboard, that you would have a pretty good idea about what was happening in the business?"

"I think I'd have a pretty good idea of what was working and what was not," Luke replied.

"And if I saw a problem in any one of these figures," Anna continued, "I could always ask for the detailed reports on which these are based to get to the bottom of things."

Taylor Construction Past Month KPI's		
Financial Highlights		
Net Profit for Current Month vs Budget	$6,852 vs $6,900	1% under budget
Net Profit Year-to-Date vs Budget	-$16,810 vs $0	Our objective is to eliminate the losses this year which we will achieve.
Cash at Bank	$53,937	
Overdue Creditors	Nil	
Overdue Debtors	$28,580	Waiting on one final payment – 15 days overdue
Marketing Highlights (for Quarter)		
New Enquiries	4	1 from Ad, 2 from architects, 1 from client referral
Quotes	3	Didn't quote on Ad enquiry
New Clients	2	1 each from architect and client referral
Operations Highlights		
Hours vs Budget	998 vs 978	2% over budget
Materials vs Budget	$58,267 vs $55,865	4% over budget

2.4 Financial Report

"Can you share the financial results with us now Anna?" asked the Advisor.

Anna placed several sheets in front of them. "This is the Financial Report."

The report included the following items:

- Profit & Loss Cash statement for the month and quarter

- Profit & Loss Accrual Statement (including committed payments and expenditures for Work-in-Progress) for the month and quarter with budget comparison

- Profit and Loss Year-to-Date with budget comparison

- Balance Sheet

- Aging Debtor report (showing how old debts are)

- Aging Creditor report

- 90 day Cash Flow Forecast

"Most of these reports I could get straight from our accounting software," Anna reported. "The Cash Flow Forecast was the one that took the longest, but I'm glad I did it because I saw a bit of a cash crunch in the third month when we have a lot of annual payments due. I'll have to manage that carefully. I've left the Gross Profit analysis to Luke."

"Just looking at this information, I can tell in minutes the financial health of the business. And as you say," Luke looked at the Advisor, "Cash is King!"

2.5 Marketing Report

"Marketing is next," stated Anna. "I've actually looked at the last 12 months because we don't handle a large number of enquiries and we can only manage two or three projects at a time. We've a pretty consistent average of 4 enquiries per quarter, but can only manage 6 projects a year, depending on the size. This means we need a sale every two months, which we're achieving, but our sales efficiency is not high. This is what I found." Anna put another sheet on the table.

"I find this rather frightening," admitted Luke. "It does take quite a while to put together a quote for a house, even with the estimating package I use. I knew that, but when you combine it with the lost sales, it is clear that we should be focusing our efforts on architects."

Referral Source	Past Clients	Architects	Other
No. Enquiries	6	5	6
Quotes	4	4	3
Sales	2	3	1
Hours per Sale (includes lost Sales)	60	40	90

"Not necessarily," responded the Advisor. "I do expect the conversion rate on non-referrals to be poorer, but not necessarily that bad. I think you could lift your conversion rates in both areas, which would require a total reconstruction of your sales process. But this is not the subject of a board discussion and I suggest we schedule a meeting dedicated to Sales Strategy and Planning. The good news is, you're not short of work, but I see there is quite an opportunity to improve here. If we get this right, it can save Luke and his estimator, if he chooses to use one, considerable time. The current average time per sale is 55 hours with an average conversion rate of your quotations of 55%. If we increased your average conversion rate to 75%, the hours per sale would be just 40 hours around a 30% improvement."

"I like the sound of that, and with that level of success, I will be a lot more enthusiastic about doing the quotes. At the moment Anna has to hound me," Luke grinned.

2.6 Operations Report

"Now I think I am the next cab off the rank with the Operations Report," Luke said. "It still needs a lot of work, but this is what I've done so far.

"We have completed three projects to date this year, so I thought I would start with them. What I've done is broken each project down into its key parts, and determined hours, labour costs and materials costs for each part and compared them with my quotations. What I found was that while my materials costs were fairly accurate, except in one project where we had soil problems, the labour costs were often quite optimistic. I've found that there are a number of areas where we take longer than I think we should."

"From your analysis, Luke," asked the Advisor, "have you been able to identify the problems?"

"I think I have. In some cases, I think some of our team require more training, and we also lose time through poor co-ordination, which is Jack's and my fault. Ultimately, it's my fault as I'm Jack's boss. Then there is some re-work because of poor communication, which I think we're already addressing. I'm working closely with Jack to address the other problems."

"Can I expect to see a Training Plan and a Co-ordination Plan at the next meeting?" asked the Advisor.

"Ah, you're worse than my mother!" Luke laughed. "Yes, of course."

2.7 Staff Performance Report

"The final report is on staff matters. Who will give that report?" asked the Advisor.

"I will," replied Anna. "We've already identified staff training as an issue, and I have noted it in the Actions List. We do have one problem still, with one of Luke's labourers, Scott. He is being less than co-operative in filling out his timesheets. I always have to chase him. I really hate doing it."

"I know this is an issue for Anna, but he is a good worker on-site, but I have told him he has to do it. I'll manage it," asserted Luke.

"Obviously I don't know Scott," said the Advisor, "but you can end up with a situation where someone who is highly productive, but doesn't comply with all procedures, perhaps cuts a few corners but still delivers, can infect other employees and affect morale. They look up to him, and perhaps he says some unfair things about 'management' behind their back. All this can create an unhealthy culture. You need to watch this carefully."

"Scott does have a bit of a mouth on him, but he is generally good natured. I will handle him," Luke insisted.

3.   New Opportunities

"Okay," observed the Advisor. "Next is New Opportunities. Anna?"

"As you said earlier, we currently have all the business we can manage, so I think as far as New Opportunities go, we just need to consolidate on what we have, and we've some marketing related actions which we should complete, making our current sales systems more effective, before we actively go looking for new business."

"I think that's right," added Luke. "I need to make the projects run more effectively before we take on any more, otherwise I'll just end up in the fire fighting game again."

"That's a sensible approach," agreed the Advisor. "However, in a future meeting I'd like to discuss a co-ordinated plan where you can grow your business, but not today. Is there any other business?"

4.   Other Business

Anna looked at Luke for a moment and then declared "I think that's enough for our first real board meeting. I just want to thank you. We've never had such a clear overview of our business, where it is, and what our priorities should be."

"We still need to work on these reports, but I can see once we have set them up, we don't need to be here to know what's going on," agreed Luke.

"I think you've done well for a first attempt at formal reporting. I am sure you'll improve the reports and make them even more useful in the future," the Advisor remarked. "The last item is to review the Action List."

Anna read out the list.

Actions List

1. Anna to bring in new assistant next month
2. Luke to investigate using an estimator to assist with quotations
3. Review criteria for giving quotations (Anna and Luke)
4. Schedule Sales Strategy and Planning Meeting (Anna)
5. Staff Training Plan (Luke)
6. Project Co-ordination Plan (Luke)
7. Implement Systems Plan (Anna and Luke)

Go to the Action Steps section for this Chapter now

Chapter 14

Team Taylor

It happened on a sunny Friday afternoon. Anna and Sally were completing the weekly reports, when Scott walked into the office. He had come to pick up some owed back-pay.

Scott was a big young man with the time spent as a labourer clearly reflected in his physique. Anna was aware that he was entering the office through vibrations of the floor. While he was generally quite friendly, Anna did feel slightly intimidated by him.

After acknowledging Sally and waving to Mark playing quietly in the next room, he turned to Anna. "Afternoon, Anna, I got your message and have just come to pick up that back-pay. Is it okay for me to collect it now?"

"That's fine, Scott. Have you got your timesheets there as I asked as well?"

"No I haven't. I'll do them next week."

"Hold on, Scott," insisted Anna firmly, "there is still an hour till knock-off time; it'll only take you 10 minutes. Here's a form, just use the spare desk."

"Look, Luke gave me the rest of the afternoon off, and I have made plans." Scott started to get aggressive.

"We've been through this before, Scott. You have to fill out the sheets before you knock-off. It's part of your job. And when you say you will do them next week, I know that means we might get them next Friday if we hassle you enough. This isn't acceptable. Sit down and fill out the forms now, and you can be on your way with your back pay in a few minutes," Anna replied with a smile.

"I don't have time for this, Anna. I have to go. Now give me my money so I can go." He glared at her, bending over her desk with hands on his hips.

"I said no," Anna said with more resolve than she felt. "Just fill in the form. You could have done it by now if you hadn't spent this time arguing with me."

"Damn you, Anna!" Scott lost his temper. "You are not the boss; you can't make me do anything."

"I am the boss. I've given you a reasonable instruction and I expect you to carry it out."

At that point Scott started swearing in a way neither Anna nor Sally a short distance away had heard before. He started pounding Anna's desk demanding his money.

Anna felt herself shaking. She had a quick look to see how Mark was. He was too young to understand what was happening, but he certainly was watching. He looked like he was about to cry. "That's it Scott. You're fired. Here's your money, now get out and never come back."

"You can't fire me Anna you ____. Luke will put you back in your place." Then after another rant, he grabbed the envelope that Anna had placed on the desk in front of him and stormed out of the office, slamming the door so hard, the walls shook.

Anna rushed over to Mark who was now crying. Sally came with her and comforted Anna when she started to cry. "I don't think I can take any more of this," Anna cried.

"The man's a brute." Sally consoled Anna. "You are well rid of him."

"I'm not sure that Luke will feel the same way. He'll be back here in an hour. I will give him the news then."

è❧

When Luke came in later, it was clear that bad news had travelled fast. "I just spoke to Scott and he was pretty angry. What on earth happened? Is it true you said he was fired?"

"Yes," murmured Anna who was clearly upset, Mark on her knee. Sally sensing a confrontation, made her way to the storeroom.

"What do you mean?" asked Luke. "Why couldn't you have called me first?"

"I had to deal with it then."

"But I need Scott. He is a hard worker," declared Luke.

"Well, no he isn't. You're better off without him – he's toxic to our business. He wanted to leave without filling in his time sheet and then he was abusive and threatening in front of Mark and Sally. If you were here, you would have thrown him out yourself."

"Well I said he could take off early because he'd done such a great job in the morning."

"I know you said he could leave early, Luke, but he refused to fill out his timesheet, something you should have made him do before he left."

Luke was standing his ground. "You need to talk to me before you do something as big as that. He wants to apologise."

"He crossed a line," Anna persisted. "I will not tolerate abuse like that from anyone, especially in front of Mark. We agreed this was to be a family friendly business. You asked me to be CEO. I did what CEOs do. Fire people who step over the line. I'm fed up of always taking the role of bad cop and I'm fed up with your boys' club. I didn't have a choice but to fire him. But you do. It's either him or me. You've got to support me on this."

Luke stood in front of Anna remaining silent. Anna stood up, carrying Mark, and walked past Luke and out of the office and headed for the house. Sally came out of the storeroom, stared at Luke for a moment, picked up her jacket and handbag, and left the office. Luke was left on his own.

When Luke walked into the house, he saw Anna in the kitchen preparing a snack for Mark. He came in and sat in a chair. "I'm sorry. You were right to fire Scott. He has more muscles than brain. I can replace him. Even though it'll put me in a spot for a bit, things will be better without him. He was becoming high maintenance. We're a team. I forgot that. The team always comes first."

Anna stood looking at Luke for a while. "Alright, if we're going to do this, we have to do it properly."

Chapter 15

The Declaration of Dependence

"**I** want to congratulate both of you on the way you came through this testing situation," the Advisor smiled. "It might not have looked pretty from your viewpoint, but I think you both got there in the end."

"I knew we would have problems with this way of working, I just didn't expect one to happen so soon. I was really angry with Luke at first," Anna said, "but I was quite proud of the way he came back and supported me. I can see it was hard for Luke too, but I think it has made us much stronger."

"I think it was the shock of getting the phone call from Scott without warning," Luke explained. "Once I understood what happened, I called him back and told him he was finished. The good thing is that the boys, as Anna likes to call them, were actually quite supportive. They always thought Scott pushed things a bit far. It has also re-enforced Anna's authority when the word had got around on what happened. The timesheets are always on time now!" Luke grinned.

"It's like a nuclear option," explained the Advisor. "You only have to show you are prepared to use it once, and you have their attention. The most important outcome is whilst under heavy fire, Team Taylor came out on top. We must now re-enforce that with a Family Charter.

"Charters are important for family businesses. They describe how you want the business to operate in a disciplined manner that minimises conflict and is supportive of family relationships. A full charter would also include how the next generation are brought into the business, what their rights are and how they can influence the direction of the business. They can contain many other policies as well such as executive performance and shareholding rights. These are complexities we should leave for another time so we can focus today on how you work together." The Advisor let his points sink in for a few seconds before continuing.

> See the Appendix for some legal considerations to protect a business against a breakdown in the personal partnership.

"What I'd like each of you to do on your own is write down a list of Do's and Don'ts that would apply to both of you. A suggested example of a 'Do' is listening carefully to the other's argument before criticising. A suggested 'Don't' is Don't criticise the other person in front of staff. Both of these are fairly obvious."

After each had finished their lists, they discussed each of the Do's and Don'ts. There was general agreement on most of the items in the list, some negotiation on a few and several more added. The Advisor then complied a single list. It started with the following declaration –

Anna and Luke agree that in Taylor Construction they will:

- Publicly support the other in front of staff, suppliers and clients

- Consult over major decisions wherever possible

- Refer back to agreed policies when making decisions

- Consult before making a decision counter to an agreed policy

- Be open and honest with each other

- Listen without interrupting as the other makes their case

- Follow through on commitments

- Give the other sufficient notice if a commitment can't be kept

- Give constructive feedback on each other's performance

- Debate not argue, based on the merits of the issue

- Call timeouts if arguments get heated

- Respect each other's role

- Commit to this Charter

They also agreed that they wouldn't:

- Criticise each other in public

- Try to do the other's job

- Micromanage the other

- Shut down debate with personal remarks

- Ignore decisions rightfully taken by the other in their role

- Use employees to reverse a decision

- Ignore issues that need to be raised

"That's a great list," announced the Advisor. "I recommend you review it from time to time to make sure that it truly reflects the way you work together and if you do have an issue, you can look at the Charter to see where you haven't complied. You both need to sign it now."

Looking at the list, Anna said "Perhaps we could have just written 'Love Honour and Obey.'"

"Yes dear" replied Luke.

Go to the Action Steps section for this Chapter now

Chapter 16

Time and Place

"Being Married to the Business is a bit like ballroom dancing" stated the Advisor. "Firstly you must be dancing to the same tune. You must also trust your partner in the lifts and lunges. While you must know where your partner is at any time, you can't dance their role for them. Your responsibility is performing your role, and be ready to catch them when the time comes.

"Once you have agreed on the tune you will dance to, your business plan, you need to give the other space to dance. There must also be space between the dances. Boundaries are important. That means you must allow for breaks, you can't be dancing or working all the time.

The Advisor paused for emphasis, "A good way to think about boundaries is: Don't treat your spouse as a business partner and don't treat your business partner as a spouse. One way of doing this is to have times and places where you are only spouses and a time where you can just be business partners. Have you set boundaries between work and life?"

"It's hard to stop working," Luke explained. "Even when we stop, we keep thinking about things and discussing what we will do tomorrow or next week."

"I'd like to stop once I walk out of our office at night, even though the office is in behind our house," Anna declared. "We need to have time where Mark is the centre of our attention, and of course time for each other."

"It will be difficult to turn off outside the office. I'm sure I'll still be thinking about what I need to organise the next day, but we can make it a rule, we stop each other if we infringe it,' Luke added.

"While you have defined your places, what about times? I imagine it is all too easy to duck out to check something in the office, only to find yourself still there an hour later," suggested the Advisor.

"All too easy," Anna agreed. "I'd like to say no work after six o'clock, and none on the weekends. I would like to say that, but it's not realistic at the moment. As a compromise, I'd still say no work after six, as I am not productive then anyway, but for a little while, I still think I need a half day on the weekend."

"I could agree to that," Luke concurred. "What doesn't get done, can wait."

"It is sensible to place definite limits," continued the Advisor. "This forces you to prioritise. Have you ever noticed whenever you have a deadline, that you can all of a sudden drop everything that was previously filling your time with little impact? That's a reflection of Parkinson's Law: Work expands to fill the time available to complete it."

"I can see that's true," observed Anna. "If I'm in the office, I'll always find something to do whether I need to do it or not. If I give myself less time in the office, I won't fill time by pottering around."

"So hold yourselves accountable for these rules, and the half day on the weekend should not be allowed to go on indefinitely," added the Advisor.

"It won't." Anna patted the rather large bulge of her waistline. "I have a fast approaching deadline."

Go to the Action Steps section for this Chapter now

Chapter 17

The Road Ahead

The Advisor declared, "I think you should chair the meeting today, Luke. How do you feel about that?"

Luke responded with little hesitation. "I feel good about that. Okay let's get started, but before we do I just want to say what a year it has been, in every sense. Quite a roller coaster ride at times, but I think that standing today looking at everything we've done, I think we should all feel proud."

"Hear hear," agreed Anna. "And of course we need to thank our Advisor."

"No, you should be congratulating yourselves," the Advisor responded. "All too often, businesses don't act on the advice they get, or only half implement it and wonder why things don't improve. To change outcomes, you have to step outside your comfort zone, which is never easy. It wasn't easy for you, but you did something many don't. You persevered."

1. Review Actions

"Alright," Luke said. "I think we'll just have to agree to disagree about this. So to the Agenda. Anna, can you let us know how the actions from the previous meeting have progressed?"

"I think we've made good progress on all action items. My new assistant, who will be supporting Sally when I take my break, has settled in well. I believe, Luke, you are very happy with your estimator."

"He's taken quite a load from my plate and he also does a great job on project reporting against budget. I hadn't appreciated that he would be able to help us there as well," agreed Luke.

"I also find it's good to have someone who's always in the office who has technical experience so we don't have to bother you as much with questions," Anna continued. "He has been a great addition to our business.

"We held our Sales Strategy and Planning meeting in which we covered quotation strategy, but I'll leave the outcomes from that to the New Opportunities agenda item.

"Luke completed a training plan for each of the on-site team which includes a mixture of on the job training and for some of the team, short courses. Everyone is pretty happy about that. Luke will report on project co-ordination later on, but progress has been made there as well. The systems development plan is on track and continuing, although I think Luke didn't realise how big a task it would be."

"It's a huge task, but I can see improvement already from some of the high priority systems which are now being used by the teams," added Luke. "They appreciate having the systems because they know what to do on key tasks without always having to find me or Jack to get an answer. And they know if they follow the system, mistakes are reduced and they won't be blamed for errors, which in all honesty, are often not their fault. Everyone is happier."

2.1 Highlights

"Do you want me to do the highlights now?" asked Anna.

"Are you doing my job now?" Luke smiled.

"No dear."

"Okay Anna, what are the highlights?" Luke said, laughing.

"The first highlight is that I feel confident with all the new systems and reporting, that Sally will be able to manage while I'm out of action, not that I'll be far away. So this will be a good test of how effective our systems are, but I'm sure that there will be no problems because I've already been able to reduce my hours steadily over the last month. Thank you Mr Parkinson.

"Next, increasing prices by just the small amount you recommended," she looked up at the Advisor, "has not impacted as far as I can see on the jobs we've won in the last few months, which of course has gone straight to our bottom line. Another highlight from Luke's area is that all new projects are meeting budget and are on time, and we're recovering from the cost blow outs on some of the older projects, which means, we have a very healthy cash flow and we will meet our year end target for monthly profit."

"Well done," remarked the Advisor.

2.2 Current Obstacles

"Any obstacles that you want to raise, Anna?" Luke inquired.

"Apart from me being unavailable, which I don't think will affect normal operations, but it may impact on our business development plans."

"I don't think it's really an issue," said the Advisor. "I will explain when we come to New Opportunities."

2.3 Key Performance Indicators Review

"Now to the reports. Key Performance Indicators Review first. Over to you Anna." Luke seemed to be enjoying his role as chair.

Taylor Construction Highlights Half Year Comparison		
Financial Highlights	**First Half Year**	**Second Half Year**
Gross Profit Margin	18%	22%
Net Profit	-$14,774	$28,375
Cash at Bank	$5,690	$61,285
Overdue Creditors	$18,740	Nil
Overdue Debtors	$53,080	$14,790
Marketing Highlights		
New Enquiries	7	8
Quotes	5	4
New Clients	3	3
Operations Highlights		
Hours vs Budget	5,960 vs 5,650 6% over budget	8,740 vs 8,800 1% under budget
Materials vs Budget	$372,396 vs $363,000 3% over budget	$422,391 vs $425,000 1% under budget

"I would like to start with a comparison of the highlights from the first half of this year with the second half. In the first half, we were just starting to turn things round, and in the second half we can see the results of all that effort."

"As you can see we have been able to increase our Gross Margin by about 20%," Anna continued. "This is due to a combination of an increase in our prices and better management of our labour hours. This has resulted in a modest Net Profit in the second half.

"While the statistics are insufficient to draw strong conclusions at this time, our conversion rate from quotes are trending in the right direction. I think this is because we're being more careful about which enquiries we respond to, but the next six months results will put us in a much better position to judge."

"A very clear presentation on how far your business has come," the Advisor declared.

2.4 Financial Report

Anna continued with her report. "I'll present all the normal reports and provide the back-up data from the highlights, but here's one special summary which I want to show. Last year compared with this year. I have adjusted last year's report to reflect the way we report data today. I've presented the differences as a percentage variance from last year.

"I've spent some time understanding the differences and after looking at the most significant changes here are my conclusions. Firstly, our sales are up due to a combination of better productivity, allowing us to take on an additional project, still underway, and of course the price increase we introduced earlier this year. The extra work resulted in increased labour and materials costs, but because of better cost control we were able to increase our margins. This would have been larger if it wasn't for all the old projects in the year.

"There were some increases in Overheads but this is mainly due to extra staff, and of course, we're paying ourselves more. Most of Luke's pay is still within Cost of Goods Sold. The full increase in office salaries will only be evident in next year's figures. I note the big change in Dues & Fees, which, of course, is due to our esteemed advisor," Anna smiled at him, "and worth every penny!"

"With an $80,000 profit turnaround even after our pay increases, I certainly second that!" agreed Luke. "But I also note quite a jump in the percentage of Telephones and IT costs."

Taylor Construction Profit & Loss			
	This Year	**Variation From Previous Year**	
		Actual	**(%)**
Sales	**1,908,533**	**+288,933**	**18%**
Labour	426,470	+41,739	11%
Subcontractors	308,220	+34,000	12%
Materials	786,730	+86,950	12%
Gross Profit	**387,114**	**+126,243**	**48%**
Overheads			
Advertising	5,890	+140	2%
Dues & Fees	34,650	+22,730	191%
Equipment Costs	7,461	+686	10%
Insurances	23,520	+1,245	6%
Labour	153,050	+22,000	17%
Office Expenses	17,908	-632	-3%
Telephones and IT	5,378	+1,128	27%
Vehicle Costs	24,860	-1,560	-6%
Vehicle Leases	56,380	0	0%
Other Expenses	14,466	+896	7%
Total Overheads	**343,563**	**+46,633**	**16%**
Depreciation	30,000		
Net Profit	**13,551**	**+79,610**	

"That's because of a combination of extra staff and more reporting," Anna explained, "but remember it's off a small base, just over a thousand dollars extra. I'm not concerned about it. Although we have these extra costs, we'll actually be making a modest net profit this year, even after paying ourselves a decent wage. Looking at the final month of the year, we actually achieved for the first time 10% net profit. I am sure we can sustain that level of profitability. In fact I am confident we will be able to exceed our budget forecast for next year."

"That's a great analysis Anna. Will you update the budget?" asked Luke.

"Yes," Anna nodded, "along with the assumptions and strategies behind them. This will become our plan for next year."

2.5 Marketing Report

"Now to the Marketing Report," Luke motioned to Anna. "Previously we agreed we would not focus on marketing until we addressed the issues around project control, because taking on new work would just damage our reputation if we couldn't deliver. I believe we have reached the point where this is no longer the significant problem that it was, and we should revisit this in the New Opportunities agenda item. As I mentioned in the Highlights, the marketing trend is positive, but otherwise the report is fairly similar to the one I presented last meeting, as expected. I table it without further comment." Anna placed the sheet of paper in front of them.

2.6 Operations Report

"I'll just provide a brief Operations Report now," Luke said. "As Anna explained in the highlights, we'll finish all new projects on time and on budget, and we're clawing back losses from the old projects. Some of them won't make much if any profit, but I don't think we will lose money on them now." He presented a sheet with the breakdown for cost to date and forecast completion cost for each project.

Luke resumed, "Training as Anna mentioned will improve future performance. It will take time to show results, but I feel I can say that our workforce will require less supervision next year than today, which will increase our capacity. This will be one of the reasons we'll be able to take on more projects next year.

"The major reasons for our results this year are the systems we are now using, and the project co-ordination planning Jack and I do whenever we take on a new project. We now have a 90 day plan for all projects and are able to move our teams around far more effectively to fit in with our specialist subcontractors and materials deliveries. This has dramatically reduced the amount of time we have men standing around waiting for something to happen before they can start their work. We're not quite 'Just in Time" yet, but it's what we want to achieve. On the skills area, Jack and I are both doing multi-project management training, which has been great for both of us. I am confident we are now in a position to take on more work.

2.7 Staff Performance Report

Luke paused, then looking at the Agenda to find his place, he asked "Anna, Staff Report?"

"We seem to have been able to recover from Scott's departure without major disruption, and his replacement seems like a nice young man. I have been told I should stop calling them 'boys'. The new assistant and the estimator have settled in very well, although the office is getting a little squashed, especially if we have visitors," Anna reported. "We'll need to look at either an extension to the office, or having to move into a leased office in a commercial district, which is not really my preference, as I like being near the house in case whoever is looking after the children needs a hand."

"A proper commercial office would be more professional than having clients come behind our home to the office," Luke agreed. "We're quite restricted on what we can do with signage. I hear what Anna says, but sooner or later if we want to grow, which I think we both do, we'll have to move out. It doesn't need to be straight away. We might be able to go for another year in this location, but I think, in that time, we should be able to find a commercial office within 5–10 minutes from here. What do you think, Anna?"

"I guess it's inevitable, and if it's a year from now, the baby will be settled and 5 or even 10 minutes away should be fine, but we can come back to this in the New Opportunities discussion."

3. New Opportunities

"Which is the next item on the Agenda." Turning to the Advisor, Luke asked, "Would you like to lead this discussion?"

"Certainly," answered the Advisor. "As we discussed earlier, your growth strategy was to be deferred so that you could address your service delivery problems, which I think you have. To plan for growth, there are two key perspectives we need to consider – Marketing and Operations, but the starting point is setting a target. How much growth do you want, and can you handle? Growth means you will need to increase your workforce. Does that mean another on-site team, another supervisor, and what are the implications for the office? Does it need to expand, and how does all this impact on your desire to have a family friendly business?"

"We can manage three projects at a time with our current staff," Luke replied. "I would like to take that to four with occasionally five as one project finishes and another starts. It'll mean a team size increase, and another supervisor. Jack and I are already grooming one of the guys to take that role.

"It will be necessary to build a new team, but there will be economies of scale. Jack and I have already discussed how we can achieve that with a new project. It's actually an assignment for our course, so we'll even have our plans marked by a project management professional! I think when Anna is back at work, we'll be able to cope without additional staff in the office."

"For the expected paperwork increase from three to four projects, our staff can probably manage without me," Anna responded. 'If our object is to manage four and a bit projects in the next 12 months, I think we can stay where we are, but if we want to grow beyond that, I agree we will have to move our office."

"Will this still be family friendly?" asked the Advisor.

"If we tried this a year ago, it wouldn't have been," Anna answered. "It'd just have meant even more hours and stress, but now we have built an infrastructure with our Business Management System, which is now a platform for future growth without the stresses we had in the past."

"If Anna feels that way, especially with a baby on the way, and we stick with our rules, I believe we can keep it family friendly," said Luke. "I can see you are about to say something," Luke looked at the Advisor, "but I know what you are going to say – that we need to document the plans we have to manage the extra work."

"You are reading my mind now," smiled the Advisor. "This brings us to marketing and sales part of the New Opportunity equation. We spent time looking at your sales processes last month, and I think we agreed with the restructured pipeline, you'll be able to achieve more sales with just the current flow of enquiries. Even allowing for those we agreed that you would not quote on in future, if you had the last 12 months over again, you would've been able to achieve your four simultaneous projects without additional marketing.

"Anna, that's why I don't think your absence will hinder your growth objectives. However, longer term, greater marketing effort will be necessary, especially if you want to increase your prices further, which I do believe is achievable. I suggest we have a Marketing Strategy meeting on your return to work, but in the meantime, you might want to read some marketing books when you feel like some mental stimulation."

"Oh, I know I'll need it," Anna said, "but at this stage I won't make any promises."

"Only if you feel up to it. Remember, keep it family friendly," repeated the Advisor. "Next we need to turn this into a budget with the extra costs matching the revenue increase. This would include the productivity increases you have already gained over the last few months. I'm sure it will look very attractive, but as you know by now, if you don't set targets against which to measure things, it just doesn't happen."

"I'll document all this," Anna noted. "I don't want it to wait until I come back, and while I'm sure Sally will do a great job, I'm not sure she's ready for this."

4. Other Business

"Any other business?" asked Luke.

"Well it's my time to thank you," answered the Advisor. "It's been a pleasure for me to see how you have both grown, not only in your business know-how but also personally. I look forward to coming back next year and seeing the new addition to your family."

"We appreciate all your help," Luke responded.

"Your encouragement was as important to us as much as your experience," Anna added.

As the Advisor stood up, he shook hands with Anna and Luke and said goodbye, and left the two of them together with their Action List.

5. Actions List

1. Anna to update budget forecast and plan for next year

2. Anna and Luke to document plans to manage increased activity for the next year

3. Luke to implement sales pipeline changes agreed at the previous workshop

4. Anna to analyse the financial implications of the new plan

5. Anna to start reading Marketing books recommended by the Advisor when she feels ready

6. Luke to become acting CEO during Anna's absence from the business

Go to the Action Steps section for this Chapter now

Epilogue

" It's great to see you again," said Bill. "It must be over a year since you were here last."

"I was so pleased when you called us," Luke replied. "It gave us an excuse to get away."

"We had to call to hear how Anna and little Jessie were going," reminded Jenny.

"Well you can see for yourself," Anna smiled. Jessie was asleep in her arms. "She's a little angel."

"You're back at work now, Anna?" asked Jenny.

"Yes I am, but I took an extra month off, because Sally was managing so well. In the end I was really keen to get back into it after we had a session on marketing strategy with our advisor."

"You are still working with him then?" asked Bill.

"Yes, but he now just comes in for our end of quarter board reviews, which is great, because it keeps us focused and he always brings a different perspective. We also have occasional strategy sessions like the one last month."

"I hear from Gail the business is going very well. She likes to keep an eye on the competition," Bill winked.

"Well, you shouldn't have told us to get an advisor," Luke mused.

"I didn't expect you to act on my advice," said Bill laughing. "Most people don't."

"I think we were so desperate at the time, if you said, consult an astrologer, we'd have done that too!" Luke smiled. "It has been an exciting year with highs and lows but it has been worth all the hard work. I think we are now where you were when I left and we started on our own."

"You have done well then," said Bill. "It took us 15 years to get to that point!"

"We have both been able to cut back on our hours and yet still have our best year ever," Anna stated. "When the new supervisor has been properly trained, and Jessie is a bit older, we plan to take regular breaks."

"What about the next generation?" asked Jenny. "Mark or Jessie?"

"Gail is a great inspiration. She inspired me in my new role. As for the next generation, the opportunity is there if they want it. You can see Mark does like his building blocks." Anna nodded towards Mark who was quietly playing with Bill and Jenny's grandchildren's toys. "As for Jessie, who knows?"

As Luke lifted Jessie carefully from Anna's arms, he declared "I can't wait to find out."

Postscript

What I have portrayed through a series of conversations are the debates that occur with couples "Married to the Business". The situations within this story are based on real events. This case study is an amalgam of many husband and wife clients from a wide range of business sectors with whom I have worked over my career as a business advisor, mentor and coach.

For some readers, the board meetings and the conversations may appear contrived, as they might expect couples "Married to the Business" to have plenty of opportunity to hold such conversations every day as they work together. Unfortunately, this is seldom the case and unless a formal occasion is created, even if that may appear a little artificial, these important conversations don't happen.

I have presented the board conversations as a mixture of the formal and informal, which is generally the case in small business. It is my intent for the reader to feel as if they are sitting in the room as observers of the meeting and to give them the questions they should be asking about their business. By listening into these meetings, I hope couples "Married to the Business" see the types of analysis they should be making, how to interpret the results, and how to make decisions based on the conclusions.

Another reason for having these formal occasions is that it forces owners to analyse performance and prepare the reports on the business.

Otherwise, it is all too easy for them to give excuses for not completing reports because they are busy.

These reports are essential for understanding business performance and uncovering issues hiding below the surface. They also allow the business to run without the couple being there every day. In a business that has partners who are not in a relationship, when one partner is away, the other can manage the business in their absence with less need for reporting as one owner can always be present to keep an eye on things. However, couples "Married to the Business" like to be away together, making reporting all that more important.

While it is of course possible to make the changes without an external advisor, it is more difficult. By having an independent advisor the artificialness of board meetings is greatly reduced. An advisor will also increase the discipline which is missing for many couples "Married to the Business". An independent person can also be a circuit breaker for conflict that might otherwise arise.

Perhaps of greatest importance to couples "Married to the Business" is their work/life balance. I hope that the conversations in this book assist them in achieving that balance.

May Your Business Be – As You Plan It!

Dr Greg Chapman

Action Steps

As this book is presented as a Case Study narrative of a couple "Married to the Business" facing issues and overcoming them, it is not always possible to make clear the specific actions they take without disrupting the flow of the story. In this section, those actions are made clear and additional materials are provided to assist couples working together to emulate the results of the couple in the case study. The materials referred to in these steps are accessible via the Resources page.

Remember, if you change nothing, nothing changes!

Chapter 3 Action Steps

1. Each partner should independently describe the business they run together as it is today. This should include what is working and what is not working.

2. Exchange the descriptions with your partner and mark those points with which you agree and those with which you don't.

3. Discuss each of the points with which you disagree providing evidence for your point of view. This could be examples or statistical data to back your point of view. Where no data exists, you may need to do some research to back your hunch, because that is all it is without data.

4. Complete your description of your business as it is today by negotiating a form of words that will bridge any remaining differences.

Chapter 4 Action Steps

1. Using the Profit & Loss template from the Resources page, enter your figures for the last 12 months.

2.1 Determine what a proper combined wage should be for the owners. This could be based on either what you believe you should earn or what you could receive if you were working for someone else. If you can't achieve even a wage that you could receive by getting a job, why on earth would you also want to take on the risk on running a business?

2.2 Using the Profit & Loss template for the Adjusted Historical Profit & Loss statement, adjust the historical wage you received with what it should be from the previous step. Where applicable, distribute this wage between Cost of Goods Sold (for service delivery) and Overhead.

2.3 Use the Depreciation Worksheet from the Resources page and determine the combined depreciation of your assets. Note this is not tax depreciation, unless it is based on asset life, and should also exclude any asset that has lease costs already included in the Profit & Loss statement. The purpose of this is to capture capital costs that are not otherwise included in the Profit & Loss statement.

2.4 Enter the average depreciation into the Adjusted Historical Profit & Loss statement.

3.1 Is your Net Profit after you have made these adjustments what you want it to be? If not, how much Net Profit do you want, express both in $'s and as a % of turnover.

3.2 Use the Profit & Loss Forecast template and modify the Sales and Costs to reach the Net Profit you desire.

4. Write down your new Net Profit objective along with your cost and sales targets. This is the starting point for your goal setting for your new business plan.

Chapter 5 Action Steps

1. Each owner should keep a diary for a week. A worksheet for the diary can be accessed via the Resources page

Chapter 6 Action Steps

1. Each owner should draw up an Importance/Urgency matrix for themselves and add activities into each quadrant from their diary. Times associated with each activity should be added next to each and totals added to determine how much time was spent in each quadrant for the week. The matrices should be shared and discussed initially to obtain agreement that this is a fair representation of the other's week.

2. Together go through the quadrants one at a time in each matrix. For Not Urgent/Not Important tasks identify ways to delegate, outsource or stop altogether the activity.

3. Activities in the Not Important/Urgent quadrant are primarily fire fighting. For each activity, determine how these fires could have been prevented. Generally this will mean developing systems to prevent the need for urgent action. This could include checklists or gathering more information earlier in the workflow process.

4. Hopefully there were few if any activities in the Important/Urgent quadrant. These are crises whose impact could be reduced in most cases through good planning and risk management. Even the consequences of lightning strikes can be mitigated with fire control systems, off-site data storage, insurance and a disaster recovery plan. If there was a crisis, consider what prior planning would have mitigated it. Longer term, a full risk identification analysis and mitigation planning should be undertaken. This is something that is Important/Not Urgent.

5. Write down an action plan, with completion times and implementation responsibility. This action plan should be reviewed regularly, and periodically a new diary kept to see how much you are increasing your time in the Business Sweet Spot quadrant.

Chapter 9 Action Steps

1. Define the reporting structure for your organisation. Describe each of the roles and who is going to fill those roles.

2. Write down how day-to-day decisions will be made by the CEO, and which decisions will be delegated.

Chapter 10 Action Steps

1. Each partner should separately create their list of what they want from the business and from their family lifestyle.

2. Exchange lists with your partner and mark those points with which you agree and those with which you don't.

3. Write down the points with which you agree.

4. Discuss each of the points with which you disagree and complete a combined list where each point is agreed.

5. Construct a joint Vision Statement from the agreed points. This is a series of statements on how both partners view the future of the business and how it supports their family ambitions.

Chapter 11 Action Steps

1. From your Vision Statement write down two-three sentences which are a summary of your:
   - Marketing Strategy
   - Operating Strategy
   - Business Strategy
   - Family Strategy

2. Together answer the following questions:
   a. What income do you both need to live comfortably now?
   b. What income would you like to have in five years time?
   c. How many hours a week would you each want to work now and in five years?
   d. How will you manage your business alongside your family duties? What time constraints does that place upon you both?
   e. What regular time off do you both want now and in five years?
   f. What other family constraints would you want placed on your business?

3. Set profit objectives for the next 12 months and in five years using the templates provided via the Resources page. Document assumptions such as sales, costs, and operating strategies to achieve these results.

4. Using the Systems List worksheets accessible via the Resources page, identify which systems are missing from your business. Prioritise those systems that are missing in your business and provide dates and responsibility for completion.

5. Using the list of Key Performance Indicators for each business area accessible from the Resources page, identify which you will use for the Financial, Marketing, Operations and Staff reports.

6. For each Key Performance Indicator determine from where the information required will be sourced. This may require the introduction of new data collection systems into the business.

7. Take 2 or 3 of the most critical Key Performance Indicators from each key business area and create a summary monthly report– no more than a single page including highlights and obstacles.

8. Start holding weekly meetings with key staff to plan the week's activity and to ensure monthly targets are met.

Chapter 12 Action Steps

1. After a month of operations where all data is collected, create your first monthly reports. This may take longer the first time round, but as you compile them look for ways to streamline the reporting. This usually involves ways of making sure the data is collected in real time so you do not have to spend a lot of time searching for records from the past 4 weeks. In many sectors, software is available to assist in this task, but it is recommended that spreadsheets or other simple recording methods be used initially so that your software needs are well understood. Too often businesses buy software and don't use it because it is too complicated for their needs.

2. Create a monthly progress report on systems implementation.

Chapter 13 Action Steps

1. Hold your first board meeting. Identify what worked and what needs improvement.

2. List actions required to make the next board meeting more effective and reduce the effort required for preparation.

Chapter 15 Action Steps

1. Separately each partner should write down lists of Do's and Don'ts on how they expect the other to behave towards them.

2. Exchange lists marking those with which you agree and identify those that require further discussion. Merge the agreed items. Negotiate those remaining that require discussion. This may require clarification and examples of what might not have worked in the past.

3. Create a final list of Do's and Don'ts with which both of you agree. You both should sign this Charter for your business.

Chapter 16 Action Steps

1. Agree some boundaries. Where does the business stop? When does the business stop? If you were not "Married to the Business" with separate jobs, these boundaries would be fairly natural. Where would they be?

2. Each partner should police these boundaries and tactfully point out to the other when they are being breached.

Chapter 17 Action Steps

1. Analyse your business performance over the past year using the Key Performance Indicators you have already chosen for your Key Business Areas. Ideally, this should be done on a quarterly basis. What conclusions can you draw from these results? What is working, what isn't?

2. Develop a plan for the next year. Break it down into quarters and identify the strategies to be implemented each quarter.

3. Each quarter in the new year review progress against your plan, and create a detailed month-by-month plan for the next quarter. This review should also determine whether your family goals are being met.

4. Document your Reporting Plan for the next 12 months.

Resources

The following tools and resources are provided at no cost to purchasers of this book and can be downloaded from the website below.

- Diary Worksheet to determine the effectiveness of work time and for completing your Importance/Urgency matrix analysis.

- Profit and Loss Templates providing the ability to undertake sensitivity analyses to set business goals such as profit, sales and cost targets. This is a critical step for business planning.

- Depreciation Worksheet to ensure that asset costs are correctly accounted for and recovered when setting financial targets.

- Systems Planning Worksheets to identify which systems need to be developed for your business and creating a plan for their implementation.

- Key Performance Indicator Worksheets for key business areas to enable a dashboard and reports for your business to be developed.

Visit: www.MarriedtotheBusiness.com.au/resources
Use the codeword: M2BResources

Share your story with us on:
 LinkedIn at www.tinyurl.com/LI-MarriedtotheBusiness

or

 Facebook at www.facebook.com/BusinessCouples

Appendix

When Business Partners Divorce by Lyn Lucas

Part 1: When it all goes Wrong

Not all business marriages have a fairy tale ending. In the event of separation or divorce, the outcome more often than not spells disaster for a co-owned business.

The decision to separate may have been brought about by the business itself, with both parties putting in long hours to make the business a success, to the point that the business takes over their lives. A more common problem is that the business may be facing financial difficulties, and this can cause enormous stress.

A further stressor arises if the couple are in business with another married couple, and there are business debts secured on both of their family homes. This can cause a disaster not only for the separating couple, but also for their business partners.

Family Law in most jurisdictions provide that a settlement between separating couples must be "fair and equitable". An assumption can be made with a long marriage (five years or more) that the assets are divided equally. However each case is different and other factors must be considered including the financial and non-financial contributions each party has made, and whether one party may have a greater future need.

These are some of the worst case scenarios, a couple in business together could face if they decided to separate and divorce:

Loss of the business

If the business is lost, this can have a huge impact on the couple, particularly if it provides their only source of income. Another concern is the impact it will have on their business partners and employees. How can the business survive?

This depends on:

- the relationship of the parties,

- the financial health of the business, and

- the value of the other assets they own.

If the parties have enjoyed a strong personal relationship and recognise that it was the stress of the business that caused a deterioration in their relationship, they may be able to continue to work together. This might depend on the role each has previously played and the hours they have physically spent in the business. It may also depend on their particular field of expertise and whether one partner's abilities are more essential to keep the business running, while the other has played more of an administrative role.

Unfortunately, these situations are not the norm, and once a decision to separate has been made, and negotiations for a property settlement begun, it becomes too difficult to continue to work together as each decides to go a separate way.

The alternatives are for the business to be sold, or for one partner to buy out the other. This decision then raises the questions of how financially healthy is the business, and what other assets the partners have to divide between them so that a fair and equitable property settlement will result.

A business valuation is essential in either scenario. This is normally done by an agreed expert valuer. If the business is sold to a third party, then the value is what the buyer is prepared to pay, but if one party is to buy out the other the valuation is a guide as to a fair sale price, and is the value used in the preparation of a Balance Sheet of the parties' assets and liabilities.

If one partner wishes to retain the business, the feasibility of buying out the other partner will depend on the value of the other assets and how they are to be divided to make the settlement fair and equitable. If it is necessary to borrow additional funds to retain the business and pay out the other partner, the borrower will need to obtain approval for a loan and show the ability to repay it.

Alternatively if there are other partners or shareholders in the business they may be able to pay out the couple for the value of their share in the business.

These alternate scenarios should be considered so as to salvage as much of the value of the business as possible as part of the asset pool.

Loss of other assets

Business debts, such as an overdraft, are usually secured on the parties' marital home, and in some cases the debt level is such that the home will need to be sold to discharge the business debts. This may have a domino effect on other business partners who have also secured a home for business loans.

If there are other loans or leases on business equipment or motor vehicles then the loss of these assets also becomes a reality.

Administration or Bankruptcy

In cases where the couple are simply unable to carry the level of debt and there are no other assets to liquidate, bankruptcy becomes the only way out. The consequential impacts on employees, suppliers and customers, not to mention the couple themselves, make this option the one of last resort.

The moral of the story is that married/de facto couples who become business partners should plan, get advice and put into place adequate steps to guard against the loss of the business, to protect the assets of the parties and save the expense of a prolonged and expensive property settlement if the relationship comes to an end.

Part 2: An Ounce of Prevention .....

It is an exciting time entering into a new business. You are passionate about the new venture and full of innovative plans for its success. But what if you are thinking of going into business with your life partner?

Before you start the business, take the time to remove the rose-coloured glasses, to ensure that you prevent the aforementioned disasters. They can be mostly avoided by taking the following simple steps when objectivity and agreement is far easier:

- Do your research,

- Get professional help, and

- Protect your assets

Do your research

Do you both share the same WHY, the same passion for starting the business and the same reasons for wanting to make it successful? Consider a consultation with a business coach or mentor to talk you through the pros and cons of starting the business, the hours you will have to spend in the business to make it a success and the capital you will need.

Discuss with your banker the funds you will be able to borrow to start the business and keep it afloat in the start-up stage, the effect of a director's guarantee and whether loans are to be secured on real estate.

Network with other business owners, talk to married couples who are in business together to get some firsthand knowledge of the hurdles you may have to overcome.

Get professional help

Consult with your accountant and/or lawyer as to the most suitable structure for the business entity. Should you have a company or a partnership? What documents should be prepared – a Shareholder's Agreement (if you are forming a Company) or a Partnership Agreement? Should you set up a Family Trust, or other means of minimising taxation?

It is strongly recommended that specialised advice is sought from a suitably qualified legal professional with business expertise operating in your jurisdiction to put these agreements in place. Discuss the benefits of these documents if your relationship breaks down in the future and how best to secure the business and your other assets in that event. This should include a process to value the business and buy-out options.

Protect your assets

More particularly in second and subsequent relationships, the parties will have already experienced a divorce property settlement, each will bring different assets into the relationship, and their financial contributions may not be equal. Steps should be taken to protect the assets you each brought into the relationship.

Finding your way through another separation and a divorce property settlement is never something you plan to happen when your partner, a person you thought you knew, becomes a person you no longer know and trust. At that time, your whole world can come crashing down, and it is difficult to know what path to follow.

To avoid this, consider a Binding Financial Agreement, or Cohabitation Agreement, entered into early in the relationship when there is love and trust between you. This is an effective way of protecting assets. Entering into such an Agreement does not demonstrate a lack of trust between partners. It is to protect the assets each of you have. These Agreements are becoming more common especially for parties entering into a second or subsequent relationship after experiencing a particularly costly and bitter property settlement with a former partner.

A Binding Financial Agreement can be signed at any time, before or during a relationship. The purpose of the Agreement is to record the assets and liabilities each of you brought into the relationship, the assets and liabilities accumulated during the relationship, and more importantly, how those assets, including a business, and liabilities are to be divided if the relationship ends.

Although there are legal costs to have the Agreement prepared, there is a huge saving of legal costs if the relationship ends because it sets out how both parties want assets and liabilities to be divided, without the need for an application to the court for a judge to make a decision. If circumstances change during the relationship, then the Agreement can be amended and redrafted at that time.

The bottom line is to treat the start of your planned enterprise with your life partner as a business decision. The Binding Financial Agreement will give both parties the confidence to put all their energies into running a successful business, rather than having a question mark as to the fate of business if the relationship should fail. The Partnership Agreement or Shareholder's Agreement can also provide the flexibility to bring in new partners or shareholders to keep the business afloat if the relationship does come to an end.

As in most matters, an ounce of prevention is worth a pound of cure.

About Lyn Lucas

Based in Newcastle NSW Australia, Lyn Lucas is a Family Lawyer with twenty years experience as a Lawyer and Mediator. Lyn has assisted hundreds of clients to resolve their family law property settlements, many of them involving a family business. Lyn's new online law practice Online Divorce Lawyer focuses solely on creating effective solutions for clients throughout Australia.

About Dr Greg Chapman

Dr Greg Chapman is a small business advisor and marketing strategist, a professional speaker and author. His first book, the best selling small business book, **The Five Pillars of Guaranteed Business Success** was a finalist in the International Indie Business Book Awards. He is the publisher of **The Australian Small Business Blog** and CEO of Empower Business Solutions.

Greg also teaches business at the University of Melbourne where his first book is on the prescribed reading list. He has also presented for such organizations as the Housing Industry Association, the Royal Australian Institute of Architects, Engineers Australia, the CPA, and the Recruitment Consultants Society of Australia as well as at industry events around the world.

His qualifications and memberships include a Ph.D. from Melbourne University, M.B.A. from Deakin University, an Australian Institute of Company Directors Diploma and he is a Certified Master Coach by Behavioral Coaching Institute and is a member of the International Coaching Council

Greg›s business experience has involved assignments in seven countries. He has been responsible for the management of businesses and projects ranging from the micro scale to billion dollar businesses. Greg lives and breathes a wide range of business solutions 'from experience'.

Find out more about Dr Greg Chapman and his business and download a complementary preview edition of "The Five Pillars of Guaranteed Business Success" at www.empowersolutions.com.au.